Michael M. Dediu

Our Future is Sustainable Peace and Prosperity

Moving from conflicts to harmony and peace

DERC Publishing House

Tewksbury (Boston), Massachusetts, U. S. A.

Published and printed in the
United States of America
On the Great Seal of the United States are included:
E Pluribus Unum (Out of many, one)
Annuit Coeptis (He has approved of the undertakings)
Novus Ordo Seclorum (New order of the ages)

Library of Congress Control Number: 2019914570

Dediu, Michael M.

Our Future is Sustainable Peace and Prosperity
Moving from conflicts to harmony and peace

ISBN-13: 978-1-939757-99-9

1-8090869861
1-3PT3F7Z
1-3PT3F86
XX2048
03958D
26KC528Q

Preface

After thousands of years of wars, violence and destruction, people say enough is enough, and ask for **Sustainable Peace, Freedom, Health, Friendship and Prosperity.**

This book is exactly about this serious problem - **shaping the future of mankind** – it has clear, precise and sharp new ideas, ready to be implemented, with plenty of aphorisms to help us do the work right, the first time ever.

Let's first remember a few excellent quotes:
Edison: I am proud of the fact that I never invented weapons to kill.
Edison: **Non-violence leads to the highest ethics, which is the goal of all evolution**. Edison: There will one day spring from the brain of science a machine or force so fearful in its potentialities, so absolutely terrifying, that even man, the fighter, who will dare torture and death in order to inflict torture and death, will be appalled, and so **abandon war forever**. Hoover: Older men declare war. But it is youth that must fight and die.
Churchill: **If you go on with this nuclear arms race, all you are going to do is make the rubble bounce.**
Reagan: **No mother would ever willingly sacrifice her sons for territorial gain, for economic advantage, for ideology.**

Clearly, we must change: it is not easy, but it is necessary, it can be done, and it will be done, especially having in mind the examples of some big successful international personalities – like Bezos, Gates, Buffett, Ortega, Carlos, Arnault, to mention a few.

Victor Hugo said "**All the forces in the world are not so powerful as an idea whose time has come**" – well, that idea is in this book!

Michael M. Dediu, Ph. D.

Tewksbury (Boston), U. S. A., 22 September 2019

USA Chicago (1833, 2.7 million): Whitehall Hotel (1927, red, right) on E. Delaware Pl., Fourth Presbyterian Church (left down, 1871)

Table of Contents

Italy, Rome (753 BC, one of the oldest continuously occupied cities in Europe, called Roma Aeterna (The Eternal City) and Caput Mundi (Capital of the World)), in Villa Borghese (1630), a monument (1905, by Lucien Pallez, donated by the French Government) to Victor Hugo (1802 – 1885, the greatest French writer (Hernani (1830, inspired opera Ernani (1844) by Giuseppe Verdi (1813-1901)), Notre-Dame de Paris (1831), Le roi s'amuse (1832, inspired opera Rigoletto (1851) by Giuseppe Verdi)), Les Misérables (1862), Les Contemplations, La Légendre des siècles)).

1 – 7.7 Billions

1- The over 7.7 billions of people on Earth are, actually, just one very big family, and everybody is repeating daily Dum spiro, spero (While I breathe, I hope), because this very big family should be living harmoniously, like the nature, as Newton describes it: Nature is exceedingly simple and harmonious with itself – Latin: Natura valde simplex est et sibi consona.

The biggest countries by population are: 1 China (1,433 Millions). 2 India (1,366 M), 3 United States (329 M), 4 Indonesia (270 M), 5 Pakistan (216 M), 6 Brazil (211 M), 7 Nigeria (200 M), 8 Bangladesh (163 M), 9 Russia (145 M), 10 Mexico (127 M).

Between the smallest countries by population are: 233 (smallest) Vatican City (799), 217 San Marino (33,860), 216 Liechtenstein (38,019), 214 Monaco (38,964), 203 Andorra (77,142).

Italy, Venezia - The south end of La Piazzetta, the south part of Piazza San Marco, with gondole, and a wedding picture of a Japanese couple.

World Centers for Population Research and Support should change location every year, with the assistance of the United Nations, and could start, for example, in Shanghai, Mumbai, New York City, Surabaya, Karachi, Sao Paulo, Lagos, Chittagong, Saint Petersburg, Ecatepec (Mexico), Hamhung (North Korea), Zurich, Dubai, Iasi, Bo (Sierra Leone), and Vatican City.

Rule 1-1: Terence: I am a man, and whatever concerns humanity is of interest to me.

Rule 1-2: It is well known that the times are changing, and we are changing with them – from Latin: Tempora mutantur, et nos mutamur in illis.

Rule 1-3: Schopenhauer: Every man takes the limits of his own field of vision for the limits of the world.

Rule 1-4: Pythagoras: Concern should drive us into action, and not into a depression.

Rule 1-5: Confucius: The more man meditates upon good thoughts, the better will be his world, and the world at large.

Rule 1-6: Change your life for the better – from Latin: Vitam mutaveris in meliores actus

2- Sustainable Peace, Liberty, Health and Prosperity

2- Therefore, there is an immediate need to organize this big 7.7 B family such that all leave healthy in a sustainable peace, liberty and prosperity, which is in demand by billions of the planet's inhabitants. They all want to strengthen humanitarian and economic ties between people, while opening new opportunities for communication and friendship between the citizens of the world. The status quo is not anymore acceptable.
World Centers for Sustainable Peace, Liberty, Health and Prosperity should change location every year, with the assistance of the United Nations, and could start, for example, in Washington, Beijing, Moscow, London, Paris, New Delhi, Islamabad, Jerusalem, Tokyo, Berlin, Rome, Pyongyang, Seoul, Abuja, Brasilia, Damascus, Kiev, Aden, Tripoli, and Vaduz.

Rule 2-1: Cicero: Freedom is a possession of inestimable value.

Rule 2-2: Thucydides: The secret to happiness is freedom... And the secret to freedom is courage.

Rule 2-3: Epictetus: Freedom is not procured by a full enjoyment of what is desired, but by controlling the desire.

Rule 2-4: A desire to resist oppression is implanted in the nature of man.

Rule 2-5: John Milton: Give me the liberty to know, to utter, and to argue freely according to conscience, above all liberties.

Rule 2-6: John Milton: None can love freedom heartily, but good men; the rest love not freedom, but license.

Rule 2-7: Sustainable peace, liberty and prosperity rule the world.

Rule 2-8: Hoover: Freedom is the open window through which pours the sunlight of the human spirit and human dignity.

Rule 2-9: For good health: buy healthy foods, cook them properly, and eat them abstemiously.

Rule 2-10: To get healthier we need mathematics, because complex biological structures and healing processes can be better comprehended only by using advanced mathematics.

Rule 2-11: Hardy: It is the mark of a truly intelligent person to be moved by statistics.

Chicago (1833): Chicago Water Works (down, 1869, was pumping station, survived fire in 1871, now base for the Lookingglass Theatre Company), Water Tower Place (right, 1976, 74 fl, 261 m), John Hancock Center (left up, 1969, 100 fl, 457 m with antenna).

3 - Inevitability

3 – Impossible? – No!
        Inevitable? – Yes!
        Here is the practical plan – it may take several years or maybe decades to implement it, but it will be, and it will work very well. The change of the status quo cannot be postponed sine die.
World Centers for Research on the Inevitability of Change for Better should change location every year, with the assistance of the United Nations, and could start, for example, in Boston, Hong Kong, Vladivostok, Oxford, Lyon, Frankfurt, Helsinki, Accra (Ghana), Reykjavik and Jakarta (Indonesia).

Rule 3-1: Hugo: All the forces in the world are not so powerful as an idea whose time has come.

Rule 3-2: Hugo: To rise from error to truth is rare and beautiful.

Rule 3-3: When too many incorrect events take place, a change for better becomes inevitable.

4 - Brothers and Sisters

4 – First – talk to each other as brothers and sisters, like in a good family – forget the old vocabulary of enemies, adversaries, etc.
<u>World Centers for Promoting a Brothers and Sisters Attitude</u> should change location every year, with the assistance of the United Nations, and could start, for example, in Canberra (Australia), Oranjestad (Aruba), Budapest, Conakry (Guinea), and Nur-Sultan (Kazakhstan).

Rule 4-1: Napoleon: Music is the voice that tells us that the human race is greater than it knows.

Rule 4-2: In life try to help yourself, your family, your friends and others. When you cannot help much, just do not create problems.

Rome (753 BC): the north side of Corte Suprema di Cassazione in Palazzo di Giustizia (1888 – 1911, 170 m by 155 m, covered with Travertine limestone), seen from Piazza Cavour.

5 - Good Family and Collaboration

5 – Start a new vocabulary based on good family, collaboration, assistance, help each other, and so on.
World Centers for Promoting Good Family and Collaboration should change location every year, with the assistance of the United Nations, and could start, for example, in Bucharest, Manila (Philippines), Lisbon, Doha (Qatar), and Brussels.

Rule 5-1: Homer: There is nothing nobler or more admirable than when a man and a woman, who see eye to eye, keep house as man and wife, confounding their enemies, and delighting their friends.

Rule 5-2: Newton: Men build too many walls and not enough bridges.

Rule 5-3: Tact is the art of making a point without making an enemy.

Rule 5-4: Sophocles: You should not consider a man's age but his acts.

Rule 5-5: All people on Earth are indebted to their parents and grandparents for living, and to their teachers for living well.

Rule 5-6: Remember, upon the comportment and work of each of us, depends the fate of all of us.

Rule 5-6: Epicurus: It is not so much our friends' help that helps us, as the confidence of their help.

Rule 5-7: Caecus: Every man is the maker of his own fortune – from Latin: ***Faber est suae quisque fortunae***.

Rule 5-8: John Milton: He who reigns within himself and rules passions, desires, and fears is more than a king.

Rule 5-9: Washington: Happiness and moral duty are inseparably connected.

Rule 5-10: Washington: A slender acquaintance with the world must convince every man that actions, not words, are the true criterion of the attachment of friends.

Rule 5-11: Washington: Associate with men of good quality, if you esteem your own reputation; for it is better to be alone than in bad company.

Rule 5-12: Hugo: A mother's arms are made of tenderness, and children sleep soundly in them.

Rule 5-13: Hugo: When grace is joined with wrinkles, it is adorable. There is an unspeakable dawn in happy old age.

Rule 5-14: Darwin: How paramount the future is to the present, when one is surrounded by children.

Rule 5-15: We all are what we are because of our parents, grandparents, other family members, friends, and good people.

Rule 5-16: All families must help their children to quickly become self-sufficient, and then the self-sufficient children must help the aging parents – this is a fundamental requirement for a sustainable and happy society.

Rule 5-17: Hoover: Children are our most valuable natural resource.

Rule 5-18: If we are over 30, we should ask not what our parents can do for us, but what we can do for our parents.

Rule 5-19: Happiness comes when you do good things for you, your family, your friends and many others.

Rule 5-20: Confucius: Without feelings of respect, what is there to distinguish men from beasts?

UK, London, from the Shard (2012, 309 m, observatory at 244 m), looking east to the Tower Bridge (1886-1894, combined bascule and suspension turreted bridge over River Thames (flowing from west (left) to east (right)), between London boroughs Tower Hamlets (north – left up) and Southwark (south – right), length 244 m, height 65 m, longest span 82 m, clearance 8 m (closed), 42 m (open)), City Hall (2002, height 45 m, center right round, for the Greater London Authority: Mayor of London and the London Assembly).

6 - Teaching

6 – The big differences between countries, which exists now, will be solved not by transfer of money, or by migration, but by teaching the less developed countries to work better, and to improve their lives.

World Centers for Teaching Structural Improvements should change location every year, with the assistance of the United Nations, and could start, for example, in Vienna, Baku (Azerbaijan), Ottawa (Canada), Ouagadougou (Burkina Faso), Copenhagen (Denmark), Djibouti, Tallinn (Estonia), and Asmara (Eritrea)

Rule 6-1: Teaching should always be performed with much care, attention and strict rules and discipline.

Rule 6-2: Aristotle: Teaching is the highest form of understanding.

Rule 6-3: Anatole France: The whole art of teaching is only the art of awakening the natural curiosity of young minds, for the purpose of satisfying it afterwards.

Rule 6-4: Euripides: When a good man is hurt, all who would be called good must suffer with him.

7 - New Form of Management

7 – For this it is necessary to have a completely new form of management of this 7.7 B family, with a new mode of operation (from Latin: modus operandi).
World Centers for Promoting a New Form of Management should change location every year, with the assistance of the United Nations, and could start, for example, in Chicago, Sochi (Russia), Nassau (Bahamas), Cotonou (Benin), and Cairo.

Rule 7-1: In this new form of management, "Each needs the help of the other" – from Latin: Alterum alterius auxilio eget.

Rule 7-2: Confucius: When a country is governed well, poverty and mean condition are things to be ashamed of. When a country is governed poorly, riches and honor are things to be ashamed of.

Rule 7-3: Around 1795, Washington wrote: "Government is not reason; it is not eloquent; it is force. Like fire, it is a dangerous servant, and a fearful master."
Over 224 years later, exactly this type of government will have to changed.

Rule 7-4: All people have hopes – the role of a good world management is to transform all those hopes in reality.

Rule 7-5: Nobody will have too much power, and all those with some limited power will be changed frequently (every 2 or 3 years).

Rule 7-6: The new world management must reexamine the roots of the world problems, find new solutions for these problems, and implement them fast and efficient.

Rule 7-7: Att the existing treaties, laws, rules and millions of regulations will be quickly reexamined, and either adapted to the new structure, or eliminated.

Rule 7-8: Clifford: Our lives are guided by that general conception of the course of things, which has been created by society for social purposes.

Rule 7-9: A small error at the beginning of a management task will produce many errors latter, therefore correcting errors is a permanent activity.

Rule 7-10: Hoover: When there is a lack of honor in government, the morals of the whole people are poisoned.

Rule 7-11: Hoover: Wisdom oft times consists of knowing what to do next.

Rule 7-12: Picasso: Action is the foundational key to all success.

Rule 7-13: When there is progress in some areas, the people must work very hard not to have regress in some other areas.

Rule 7-14: Solutions for many problems can be found with mathematical analysis and medical help.

Rule 7-15: All the bad things done by people have a medical explanation.

Rule 7-16: The bad people need medical help, not prison. From prisons they usually come out worse, and they convince others to be bad. From specialized hospitals, there is a chance to cure them, and then they will pay the bill for treatment.

Rule 7-17: Creativity comes from observation, knowledge and thinking at square.

8 - New, Simple 10 Regions of the World

8 – First, it is urgently necessary to administratively divide this 7.7 B family in new, simple 10 regions – not the old countries with their permanent conflicts at those old borders.

World Centers for Promoting 10 New Regions should change location every year, with the assistance of the United Nations, and could start, for example, in Miami, Wuhan (China), Irkutsk (Russia), Cambridge (UK), Grenoble (France), Kolkata (India) and Khartoum (Sudan).

Rule 8-1: There is need for good decisions, knowing from Napoleon: Nothing is more difficult, and therefore more precious, than to be able to decide.

Paris - The central part of the façade of L'Opéra de Paris (1875): composers Daniel Auber (1782–1871, left), Ludwig van Beethoven (1770–1827, second), Wolfgang Amadeus Mozart (1756–1791, center) and Gaspare Spontini (1774–1851, right).

9 - R0, R1,..., R9 Delimited by Meridians

9 – The new 10 regions, called R0, R1,…, R9, should be delimited by meridians (or line of longitudes), with the assistance of the United Nations, each region having a pair of capitals (which will change every year), for example:

R0 between meridians 0 and 15^0 E, capitals: Bern and Libreville (Gabon)

R1: 15^0 E - 30^0 E, Warsaw (Poland) and Pretoria (South Africa)

R2: 30^0 E - 45^0 E, Moscow and Cairo

R3: 45^0 E - 75^0 E, Astana (Kazakhstan) and Karachi (Pakistan)

R4: 75^0 E - 85^0 E, New Delhi (India) and Tomsk (Russia)

R5: 85^0 E   - 100^0 E, Kuala Lumpur (Malaysia) and Quanzhou (China)

R6: 100^0 E - 115^0 E, Jakarta (Indonesia) and Beijing

R7: 115^0 E - 180^0, Tokyo and Sydney (Australia)

R8: 180^0 - 70^0 W, Washington and Mexico City

R9: 70^0 W – 0, Halifax (Canada) and Brasilia

10 – 770,000,000 People in Each Region

10 – Because it is desirable to have around 770 M people in each region, the meridians will have to be adjusted a few degrees east or west, with the assistance of the United Nations. The decisions will be taken by the local administrators from the 20 cities (10 pairs of capitals) mentioned at point 9. These decisions are temporary, until the election of the new management, with the assistance of the United Nations.

UK, Cambridge, a bas-relief on the eastern wall of the western building of the Old Court (1451) of Queens' College (1448), University of Cambridge, 60 m east of the Mathematical Bridge (1749).

11 - Regions Divided in 10 Sub-regions

11 – Each region will be divided by meridians in 10 sub-regions S00,   , S99, each with about 77 M people, and so on, with the assistance of the United Nations. Again, temporary decisions by the local managers from the cities at point 9, until the elections.

The north side of the Royal Observatory (1676), and the 38-inch (965.2 mm) Telescope Dome (left up), and meridian 0 to the right.

12 - Basic Structure

12 - The basic structure of the big 7.7 B family is the usual family: father, mother and two children. Ten such families will form a neighborhood, 10 neighborhoods will be a sector, 10 sectors a small city, and so on.

World Centers for Promoting the Basic Structure should change location every year, with the assistance of the United Nations, and could start, for example, in Sofia (Bulgaria), Gitega (Burundi), Santiago (Chile), Havana (Cuba), Addis Ababa (Ethiopia), and Amsterdam.

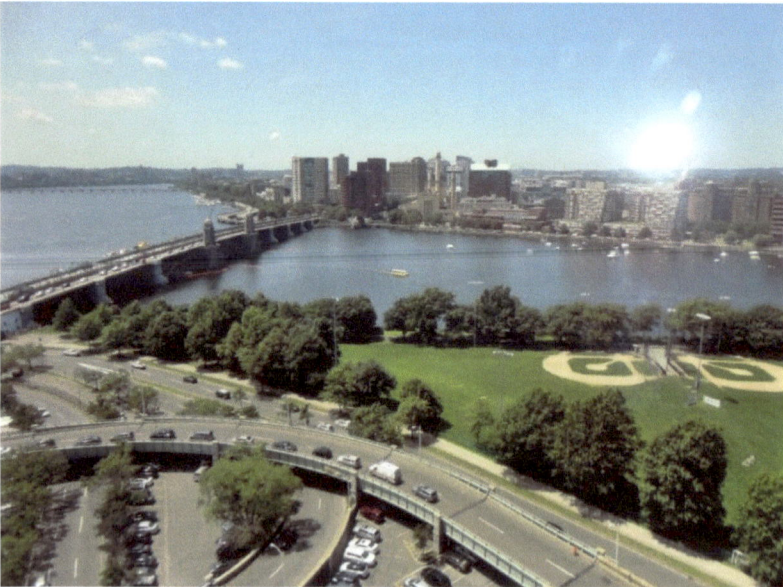

USA, Boston (1630): Charles River Basin (water flowing from left to right, into Atlantic Ocean), with Longfellow Bridge (1900-1906, 539 m) carrying Route 3 and the Red Line metro between Boston (down, Lederman Park (right)) and Cambridge (up, MIT (left)).

13 - Merit

13 – The management of this simple administrative division of the big 7.7 B family will be elected from the neighborhood up, based on merit appreciated by the people, not on political parties, or propaganda, etc., with the assistance of the United Nations.
World Centers for Promoting Elections by Merit Only should change location every year, with the assistance of the United Nations, and could start, for example, in Oslo (Norway), Lima (Peru), Volgograd (Russia), San Marino, Singapore, Manchester (UK), Ankara (Turkey), and Macao (China).

Rule 13-1: No fundraising, no donations asked by e-mails, phone calls, or mail, no begging of any type.

Rule 13-2: Civilized addressing – To John Smith, never address Hey John (how some companies wrongly do), but only Dear Mr. Smith.

Rule 13-3: Leadership is important for getting good results; therefore, much attention should be paid when electing leaders.

Rule 13-4: Cicero: Thou shouldst eat to live; not live to eat.

Rule 13-5: Tacitus: Reason and judgment are the qualities of a leader.

Rule 13-6: All managers must have strong desire to succeed in the tasks given to them by the people.

Rule 13-7: Aesop: Better be wise by the misfortunes of others than by your own.

14 - Top Management has 10 Advisers

14 – The top management will be formed of 10 Advisers, elected from the 10 regions, and each of them will be the First Adviser (***First among equals*** – from Latin: Primus inter pares) for one month, by rotation. They will move each month from a first capital of a region to the second capital of another region, at random (or based on urgency, if an emergency occurred). After this very good work, the United Nations will change into World Police and Assistance Organization, to help local police in case of big natural disasters or big accidents, and will report to the top 10 Advisers.

Rule 14-1: When Advisers make mistakes, they should promptly say mea culpa (my fault).

Rule 14-2: Advisers are not politicians, because, according to Churchill: A politician needs the ability to foretell what is going to happen tomorrow, next week, next month, and next year. And to have the ability afterwards to explain why it didn't happen.

Rule 14-3: Advisors will work hard to avoid of having what Plato said: Democracy passes into despotism. Dictatorship naturally arises out of democracy, and the most aggravated form of tyranny and slavery out of the most extreme liberty. Excess generally causes reaction, and produces a change in the opposite direction, whether it be in the seasons, or in individuals, or in governments.

Rule 14-4: Plato: Good actions give strength to ourselves, and inspire good actions in others.

Rule 14-5: Plato: Our object in the construction of the state is the greatest happiness of the whole, and not that of any one class.

Rule 14-6: Horace: Remember to maintain a calm mind while doing difficult tasks – from Latin: Aequam memento rebus in arduis servare mentem.

Rule 14-7: The Earth has to have a unified, polite and competent top management, who will provide real and strong benefit for everybody.

Rule 14-8: Schopenhauer: Wealth is like sea-water; the more we drink, the thirstier we become; and the same is true of fame.

Rule 14-9: Churchill: It's not enough that we do our best; sometimes we have to do what's required.

Rule 14-10: Churchill: Criticism may not be agreeable, but it is necessary. It fulfills the same function as pain in the human body. It calls attention to an unhealthy state of things.

Rule 14-11: De Gaulle: A true leader always keeps an element of surprise up his sleeve, which others cannot grasp, but which keeps his public excited and breathless.

Rule 14-12: De Gaulle: Faced with crisis, the man of character falls back on himself. He imposes his own stamp of action, takes responsibility for it, makes it his own.

Rule 14-13: De Gaulle: I have come to the conclusion that politics are too serious a matter to be left to the politicians.

Rule 14-14: De Gaulle: In order to become the master, the politician poses as the servant.

Rule 14-15: De Gaulle: Nothing great will ever be achieved without great men, and men are great only if they are determined to be so.

Rule 14-16: De Gaulle: Since a politician never believes what he says, he is quite surprised to be taken at his word.

Rule 14-17: De Gaulle: To govern is always to choose among disadvantages.

Rule 14-18: Aesop: It is thrifty to prepare today for the wants of tomorrow.

Rule 14-19: Aesop: United we stand, divided we fall.

Rule 14-20: Confucius: The superior man is modest in his speech, but exceeds in his actions.
The superior man makes the difficulty to be overcome, his first interest; success only comes later.
When anger rises, think of the consequences.
When it is obvious that the goals cannot be reached, don't adjust the goals, adjust the action steps.
When we see persons of worth, we should think of equaling them.
I hear and I forget. I see and I remember. I do and I understand.
To practice five things under all circumstances constitutes perfect virtue; these five are gravity, generosity of soul, sincerity, earnestness, and kindness.
The real fault is to have faults and not amend them.

Japan, north-west of the Sendai Station (1887), on Ekimae Dori, the restaurant Rigoletto, named after the famous opera with the same name, by Giuseppe Verdi (1813 – 1901), who wrote 37 operas, Rigoletto being the 17th, with the premiere at Teatro La Fenice, Venezia, on 11 March 1851.

15 – Tool, World Library

15 - Algorithmic Governance will be an essential tool for a better and impartial governing of the world, used by the Advisers selected by people. A World Library will include the Library of Congress and all the other great libraries – they will remain where they are now, but will be digitally interconnected, and accessible from any place in the world. Mathematicians from all countries will work to improve the Algorithmic Governance, to better serve the people.

Rule 15-1: Marcus Aurelius: Because a thing seems difficult for you, do not think it impossible for anyone to accomplish.

Rule 15-2: Hugo: A library implies an act of faith.

Rule 15-3: Hugo: A man is not idle because he is absorbed in thought. There is a visible labor, and there is an invisible labor.

Rule 15-4: The world library should contain a section of smart solutions and best practices designed to help all the regions of the world, to implement world projects.

Rule 15-5: Mathematical analytics could enable proactive error-finding, and ensure optimized management performance, by measuring the end-to-end quality of experience. Also, it could proactively detect security and performance issues.

16 - Medical Assistance

16 – Medical assistance will be applied to those who don't respect the rules established by people. They will work with police and other assistants.

World Centers for Medical Assistance should change location every year, with the assistance of the United Nations, and could start, for example, in the capitals mentioned at point 9.

Rule 16-1: The first rule for everybody on Earth comes from the Hippocratic Oath: Primum non nocere - first do not harm.

Rule 16-2: Balzac: Solitude is fine, but you need someone to tell you that solitude is fine.

Japan, Kawaguchiko: the bronze symbol statue "Source", by Seibo Kitamura; the vase represents Lake Kawaguchi, the woman on the left represents "positive", and the other one "negative".

17 - Collaboration Experts

17 – All lawyers will become strong collaboration experts, making sure that there are no conflicts.
World Centers for Collaboration Experts should change location every year, with the assistance of the United Nations, and could start, for example, in the capitals mentioned at point 9.

Rule 17-1: Edison: Being busy does not always mean real work. Seeming to do is not doing.

Rule 17-2: Edison: The value of an idea lies in the using of it.

Rule 17-3: Edison: There is far more opportunity than there is ability.

Rue Soufflot (from Panthéon, looking north-west to Jardin du Luxembourg (1612, back), and Tour Eiffel (1889, 324 m)), with the Université Paris 1 Panthéon-Sorbonne (1150, 1971, right).

18 – Home Visits

18 – Medical doctors and assistants will make regular home visits to all people, to keep them healthy, and to prevent illnesses.
World Centers for Home Visits should change location every year, with the assistance of the United Nations, and could start, for example, in the capitals mentioned at point 9.

Rule 18-1: This is the objective: Juvenal: A sound mind in a sound body – from Latin: Mens sana in corpore sano.

Rule 18-2: Also, everybody should have in mind:
Plato: Attention to health is life's greatest difficulty.
Ovid: There is no such thing as pure pleasure; some anxiety always goes with it.
Ovid: What is without periods of rest, will not endure.

Rule 18-3: For better health it is necessary to have a quiet atmosphere around people.

Rule 18-4: Hippocrates: Wherever the art of medicine is loved, there is also a love of humanity.

Rule 18-5: Voltaire: Men who are occupied in the restoration of health to other men, by the joint exertion of skill and humanity, are above all the great of the Earth. They even partake of divinity, since to preserve and renew is almost as noble as to create.

19 - Only Peace and Freedom Activities

19 – All military activities will become only peace and freedom activities, oriented only to help people, to build homes, schools, hospitals, roads, bridges, etc.

World Centers for Peace Related Transformations should change location every year, with the assistance of the United Nations, and could start, for example, in the capitals mentioned at point 9.

Rule 19-1: Hugo: He, who opens a school door, closes a prison.

Italy, Venezia, Giardinetti Reali, Procuratie Nuove (left), Libreria, Campanile, Basilica, San Theodore and Lion Columns, Palazzo Ducale (right).

20 – Only Civilian Purposes

20 – No armaments of any type will exist – all the military budgets in the world will go to only civilian purposes.
World Centers for Complete and Verified Disarmament should change location every year, with the assistance of the United Nations, and could start, for example, in the capitals mentioned at point 9.

France, Paris: The Panthéon (1758 - 1790, 83 m height, mausoleum in the Latin Quarter in Paris, modeled on the Pantheon (126 AD) in Rome), seen from Rue Soufflot, near Rue Saint-Jacques.

21 - International Friendship

21 - Sunday, August 4 – International Friendship Day – will be extended to all days.

World Centers for Promotion of International Friendship should change location every year, with the assistance of the United Nations, and could start, for example, in the capitals mentioned at point 9.

Rule 21-1: All the public work is *Not for me, not for you, but for us* – from Latin: Non mihi, non tibi, sed nobis.

Rule 21-2: Let us refrain from erring – from Latin: Festinamus errare.

Switzerland, Geneva (121 BC under Romans, 375 m elevation), United Nations building seen from Avenue de la Paix.

22 - People Want Sustainable Peace and Freedom

22 - People want sustainable peace, freedom, health, friendship and prosperity.

World Centers for Promoting Peace, Freedom, Health, and Prosperity should change location every year, with the assistance of the United Nations, and could start, for example, in the capitals mentioned at point 9.

Rule 22-1: People who complain of everything, and always, should be asked to work hard to help resolve their complains, and then take a break from complaining.

Rule 22-2: Stendhal: Life is too short, and the time we waste in yawning never can be regained.

Rule 22-3: Balzac: It is easy to sit up and take notice; what is difficult is getting up and taking action.

USA, Newport (1639): The west site of the Elms, 1899 - 1901, Edward Julius Berwind (1848 – 1936), inspired from Château d'Asnières (1753) in Asnières-sur-Seine (1158, 7.9 km northwest of the center of Paris, France).

23 - Transform All Deadly Tasks into Healthy Tasks

23 - In the history of mankind, much more money, time and energy was wasted on destructive and deadly tasks (war related), than on constructive and healthy ones (improving people's quality of life) – this is not acceptable anymore - people in all countries ask for a complete change: transform all destructive and deadly tasks into constructive and healthy ones.

World Centers for Transforming Destructive Activities into Constructive Activities should change location every year, with the assistance of the United Nations, and could start, for example, in the capitals mentioned at point 9.

Rule 23-1: Reagan: No mother would ever willingly sacrifice her sons for territorial gain, for economic advantage, for ideology.

Rule 23-2: Edison: I am proud of the fact that I never invented weapons to kill.

France, Lyon (43 BC), part of eastern façade of the Hôtel de Ville (1645 – 1651, 1674) de Lyon, in Place de la Comédie, across Opéra.

24 – Only Non-violent Means

24 - The management of the world will be only through non-violent means.
World Centers for Creating a Non-Violent Atmosphere should change location every year, with the assistance of the United Nations, and could start, for example, in the capitals mentioned at point 9.

Rule 24-1: Aristotle: It is the mark of an educated mind to be able to entertain a thought without accepting it.

Rule 24-2: Cicero: One should employ restraint in his jests.

Rule 24-3: Sometimes it appears that there is no hope, but "dum vita est spes est" (while there is life, there is hope).

Rule 24-4: It is a permanent requirement: Not to injure other – from Latin: Alterum non laedere.

Rule 24-5: Herodotus: Force has no place where there is need of skill.

Rule 24-6: Mark Twain: The human race has one really effective weapon, and that is laughter.

25 – Sustainable Peace Structure

25 – We will inspire from the best experiences and knowledge of all the current countries, to build this SPEFHAP (Sustainable PEace, Freedom, HeAlth and Prosperity) or Sustainable Peace Structure. **World Centers for Creating Sustainable Peace, Freedom, Health, and Prosperity** should change location every year, with the assistance of the United Nations, and could start, for example, in the capitals mentioned at point 9.

Rule 25-1: Everybody should remember:

Giordano Bruno: Truth does not change because it is, or is not, believed by a majority of the people.

Cicero: According to the law of nature it is only fair that no one should become richer through damages and injuries suffered by another.

Cicero: Gratitude is not only the greatest of virtues, but the parent of all the others.

Cicero: Nature has planted in our minds an insatiable longing to see the truth.

Cicero: Never go to excess, but let moderation be your guide.

Cicero: Faithfulness and truth are the most sacred excellences and endowments of the human mind.

Rule 25-2: Jefferson: A wise and frugal Government, which shall restrain men from injuring one another, which shall leave them otherwise free to regulate their own pursuits of industry and improvement, and shall not take from the mouth of labor the bread it has earned. This is the sum of good government, and this is necessary to close the circle of our felicities.

Rule 25-3: Anatole France: If a million people say a foolish thing, it is still a foolish thing.

26 - Free Market Economy

26 – For economy it is clear that the free market economy gives the best results, with just a few part-time independent assistants and monitors, to make sure that there are not abuses. Sine qua non requirements for happiness are morality and free market.
World Centers for Promoting Free and Correct Market Economy, as well as Morality should change location every year, with the assistance of the United Nations, and could start, for example, in the capitals mentioned at point 9.

Rule 26-1: Balzac: There is no such thing as a great talent without great will power.

Rule 26-2: Hoover: Competition is not only the basis of protection to the consumer, but is the incentive to progress.

Rule 26-3: Hoover: It is just as important that business keep out of government, as that government keep out of business.

Rule 26-4: Hoover: Prosperity cannot be restored by raids upon the public Treasury.

48

27 – Part-time unarmed police

27 – Part-time unarmed police will be necessary for accidents and other emergencies – they will work with the medical system and with volunteers.

World Centers for Assisting Part-time Unarmed Police should change location every year, with the assistance of the United Nations, and could start, for example, in the capitals mentioned at point 9. They will help to find part-time jobs for those who are not full-time police – the idea is that the people will become much better, and not too much police will be needed.

Rule 27-1: Pythagoras: No man is free, who cannot control himself.

Japan, Kobe (201 AD, the 5th largest city in Japan, 30 km west of Osaka): inside the Sogo store, located in Hanshin Railway Sannomiya Station, on Flower Road, the customers can see beautiful decorations for Christmas 2008 in Kobe.

28 – Education

28 – Education is important – teachers will work with parents and grandparents, to educate the children to leave healthy in a sustainable peace, liberty and prosperity. Discipline must be strict, and those who do not behave properly, will get medical assistance. **World Centers for Promoting Good Education and Discipline** should change location every year, with the assistance of the United Nations, and could start, for example, in the capitals mentioned at point 9.

Rule 28-1: People know very well that *As you sow, so shall you reap* – from Latin: Ut sementem feceris ita metes.

Rule 28-2: Aristotle: The roots of education are bitter, but the fruit is sweet.

Rule 28-3: Plato: Ignorance, the root and stem of all evil.

Rule 28-4: Plato: Let parents bequeath to their children not riches, but the spirit of reverence.

Rule 28-5: Plato: No man should bring children into the world, who is unwilling to persevere to the end in their nature and education.

Rule 28-6: Plato: There is no harm in repeating a good thing.

Rule 28-7: Plato: We ought to esteem it of the greatest importance, that the fictions, which children first hear, should be adapted in the most perfect manner to the promotion of virtue.

Rule 28-8: Beethoven: Recommend to your children virtue; that alone can make them happy, not gold. I speak from experience

Rule 28-9: Cicero: A home without books is a body without soul.

USA, Cambridge: 1 Feb 2010, geometrical shapes presented at MIT Mathematics Department, including octahedrons (left up, with 8 faces, 12 edges and 6 vertices; a regular octahedron has equilateral triangles for its faces, and is one of the 5 platonic solids), dodecahedrons (with 12 faces, 30 edges and 20 vertices; a regular dodecahedron has regular pentagons for its faces, and is one of the 5 platonic solids), icosahedron (with 20 faces, 30 edges and 12 vertices; all the faces are triangles; a regular icosahedron is one of the 5 platonic solids with all faces being equilateral triangles).

Rule 28-10: Cicero: Cultivation to the mind is as necessary as food to the body.

Rule 28-11: Solon: I grow old learning something new every day.

Rule 28-12: Archimedes: There are things which seem incredible to most men who have not studied Mathematics.

Rule 28-13: Cicero: There are more men ennobled by study than by nature.

Rule 28-14: Cicero: What nobler employment, or more valuable to the state, than that of the man who instructs the rising generation?

Rule 28-14: Cicero: They condemn what they do not understand – from Latin: *Damnant quodnon intelligunt.*

Rule 28-15: Seneca: Men learn while they teach – from Latin: *Homines dum docent discunt.*

Rule 28-16: Quintilian: For the mind is all the easier to teach before it is set.

Rule 28-17: Quintilian: We must form our minds by reading deep rather than wide.

Rule 28-18: Leonardo da Vinci: Learning never exhausts the mind.

Rule 28-19: John Milton: A good book is the precious lifeblood of a master spirit.

Rule 28-20: John Milton: The superior man acquaints himself with many sayings of antiquity and many deeds of the past, in order to strengthen his character thereby.

Rule 28-21: Lambert: I understood that the will could not be improved before the mind had been enlightened.

Rule 28-22: Jefferson: Books constitute capital. A library book lasts as long as a house, for hundreds of years. It is not, then, an article of mere consumption but fairly of capital, and often in the case of professional men, setting out in life, it is their only capital.

Rule 28-23: Goethe: All intelligent thoughts have already been thought; what is necessary is only to try to think them again.

Rule 28-24: Lincoln: Books serve to show a man that those original thoughts of his aren't very new at all.

Rule 28-25: Mark Twain: The man, who doesn't read good books, has no advantage over the man who can't read them.

Rule 28-26: Anatole France: An education isn't how much you have committed to memory, or even how much you know. It's being able to differentiate between what you know, and what you don't.

Rule 28-27: Dediu: Few people know,
            How much you have to know,
            To know,
            How little you know.

Rule 28-28: Be hungrier for knowledge than for food.

Rule 28-29: Even a drop of education can change the color of an ocean of ignorance.
Computers are tools for education, not substitutes of it.

Rule 28-30: Newton: I do not know what I may appear to the world; but to myself I seem to have been only like a boy playing on the seashore, and diverting myself now and then finding a smoother pebble or a prettier shell than ordinary, whilst the great ocean of truth lay all undiscovered before me.

Rule 28-31: Voltaire: A human being is not attaining his full heights until he is educated.

Rule 28-32: Descartes: The reading of all good books is like a conversation with the finest minds of past centuries.

Rule 28-33: Confucius: You cannot open a book without learning something.

USA, Chicago (1833): Fourth Presbyterian Church (right center, 1871), Elysées Condominiums (center-right, 1972, 56 floors, 161 m), Loyola University of Chicago (red center down, 1870, 1927 this building), Park Tower (center-left, 2000, 67 floors, 257 m).

29 – Science and Technology

29 – All technology – including computers, e-mails, robots, etc. – will be used only for SPEFHAP (Sustainable PEace, Freedom, HeAlth and Prosperity) purposes. All abusers, cybercriminals, etc. will be medically assisted, until they become good people. **World Centers for Creating Completely Safe, Polite and Civilized Internet and Technology** should change location every year, with the assistance of the United Nations, and could start, for example, in the capitals mentioned at point 9.

Rule 29-1: Plato: This City is what it is because our citizens are what they are.

Rule 29-2: Plato: We ought to fly away from Earth to heaven as quickly as we can; and to fly away is to become like God, as far as this is possible; and to become like him is to become holy, just, and wise.

Rule 29-3: Seneca: There is no easy way from the Earth to the stars – Latin: Non est ad astra mollis e terris via.

Rule 29-4: Poincare: It is far better to foresee even without certainty, than not to foresee at all.

Rule 29-5: Data, mathematical modeling and simulations are critical to planning for, and maintaining sustainable communities all over the world.

Rule 29-6: Niels Bohr: Technology has advanced more in the last thirty years than in the previous two thousands. The exponential increase in advancement will only continue.

Rule 29-7: Caesar: Creating is the essence of life.

Rule 29-8: Beethoven: There are not barriers erected, which can say to aspiring talents and industry, "Thus far and no farther."

Rule 29-9: J. S. Mill: All good things which exist are the fruits of originality.

Rule 29-10: All forms of art which help people are welcome.

Rule 29-11: Pasteur: In the field of scientific observation, chance favors only the prepared mind.

Rule 29-12: Cantor: The essence of mathematics lies in its freedom.

Rule 29-13: Clifford: An atmosphere of beliefs and conceptions has been formed by the labors and struggles of our forefathers, which enables us to breathe amid the various and complex circumstances of our life.

Rule 29-14: Clifford: If a belief is not realized immediately in open deeds, it is stored up for the guidance of the future.

Rule 29-15: Clifford: It is wrong always, everywhere, and for anyone, to believe anything upon insufficient evidence.

Rule 29-16: Clifford: No simplicity of mind, no obscurity of station, can escape the universal duty of questioning all that we believe.

Rule 29-17: Poincaré: It is through science that we prove, but through intuition that we discover.

Rule 29-18: Poincaré: Mathematical discoveries, small or great, are never born of spontaneous generation.

Rule 29-19: Poincaré: Mathematicians are born, not made.

Rule 29-20: Poincaré: To doubt everything, or, to believe everything, are two equally convenient solutions; both dispense with the necessity of reflection.

Rule 29-21: Poincaré: One would have to have completely forgotten the history of science, so as to not remember that the desire to know nature has had the most constant, and the happiest influence on the development of mathematics.

Rule 29-22: Whitehead: Civilization advances by extending the number of important operations, which we can perform without thinking of them.

Rule 29-23: Hoover: New discoveries in science will continue to create a thousand new frontiers for those who still would adventure.

Rule 29-24: Picasso: Art washes away from the soul the dust of everyday life.
We don't grow older, we grow riper.
Work is a necessity for man. Man invented the alarm clock.
Youth has no age.

Rule 29-25: Banach: Mathematics is as old as Man.
Mathematics is the most beautiful and most powerful creation of the human spirit.

Rule 29-26: Innovation is applied creativity.

Rule 29-27: Science and technology are the engines of progress.
The Internet is like a huge library – keep it clean and unpolluted.

30 - World Constitution

30 – Inspiring from a well-known document, we can write now the World Constitution:

We the People on this Earth, in order to form a Structure with Sustainable Peace, Freedom, Health, Friendship and Prosperity on our beloved Earth, establish this Constitution for the World.

Rule 30-1: The safety and wellbeing of the people are the highest priority.

Rule 30-2: Goethe: Which government is the best? The one that teaches us to govern ourselves.

Rule 30-3: Goethe: Wisdom is found only in truth.

Rule 30-4: Washington: The basis of our political system is the right of the people to make and to alter their constitutions of government.

31 - Rules on our Earth

31 - <u>**All the rules on our Earth will be established by people and their elected Advisers**</u>, therefore it is normal to act ad amussim (according to a rule).

Rule 31-1: It is good to have in mind these:
Pythagoras: As soon as laws are necessary for men, they are no longer fit for freedom
Tacitus: In a very corrupt state are the most laws - from Latin: Corruptissima re publica plurimae leges

Rule 31-2: Cato the Elder: Patience is the greatest of all virtues.

Rule 31-3: Quintilian: Everything that has a beginning comes to an end.

Rule 31-4: Pliny the Younger: However often you may have done them a favor, if you once refuse, they forget everything except your refusal.

Rule 31-5: Dante: A fair request should be followed by the deed in silence – from Italian:
> *La dimanda onesta*
> *si de' seguir con l'opera tacendo.*

Rule 31-6: The Earth is better governed if it has few rules, and those rules are strictly observed.

Rule 31-7: Descartes: Except our own thoughts, there is nothing absolutely in our power.

Rule 31-8: Descartes: It is only prudent never to place complete confidence in that by which we have even once been deceived.

Rule 31-9: Voltaire: Work saves us from three great evils: boredom, vice and need.

Rule 31-10: Edison: Hell, there are no rules here - we're trying to accomplish something.

Rule 31-11: Euripides: Experience, travel — these are an education in themselves.

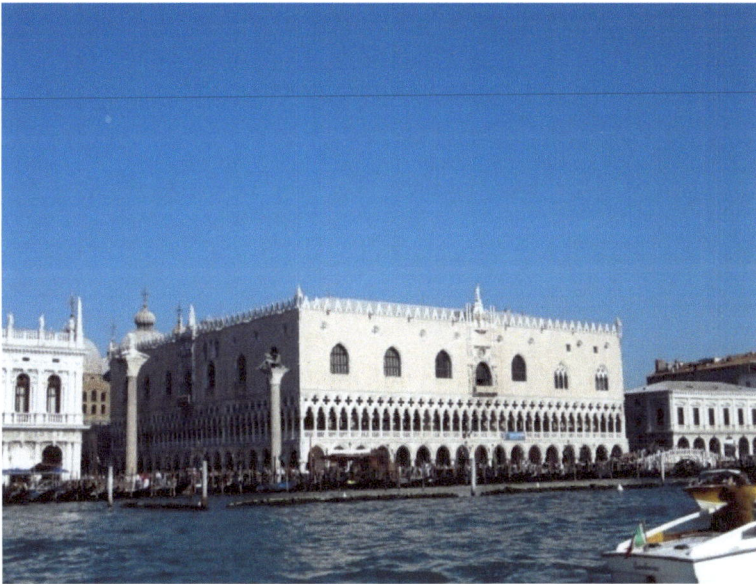

Venezia: Libreria (left), San Theodore Column, Palazzo Ducale, Lion of Venice Column (center) on Riva degli Schiavoni street.

32 - Elected every 20 months for one term only

32 – **<u>The Advisers should be elected every 20 months for one term only.</u>** If an Adviser X was elected for a term T1, then the next term T2 will have another Advisor Y. For the next term T3, X can be elected again, but the next term T4 will have a new Adviser, and so on. **<u>An Advisor can be elected, not consecutively, at most 4 times</u>** (80 months = 6 years and 8 months).

Rule 32-1: Seneca: To govern is to serve, not to rule.

Rule 32-2: Sophocles: There is no greater evil than anarchy.

Rule 32-3: Tacitus: A desire to resist oppression is implanted in the nature of man.

Rule 32-4: Solon: Learn to obey before you command.

Rule 32-5: Solon: Put more trust in nobility of character than in an oath.

Rule 32-6: Solon: In giving advice seek to help, not to please, your friend.

Rule 32-7: Aesop: It is thrifty to prepare today for the wants of tomorrow.

Rule 32-8: Democritus: It is greed to do all the talking but not to want to listen at all.

Rule 32-9: Hippocrates: Everything in excess is opposed to nature.

Rule 32-10: Hippocrates: Make a habit of two things: to help; or at least to do no harm.

Rule 32-11: Balzac: Power is action; the electoral principle is discussion. No political action is possible when discussion is permanently established.

Rule 32-12: Marcus Aurelius: If it is not right, do not do it; if it is not true, do not say it.

Switzerland, Geneva (121 BC under Romans), Avenue de la Paix 19, International Committee of the Red Cross, founded by Jean Henri Dunant (1828-1910) on Feb. 9, 1863, three Nobel Peace Prizes.

33 - Minimum age 25 years

33 – **Advisers' minimum age should be 25 years.**

Rule 33-1: Seneca: Let us train our minds to desire what the situation demands.

Rule 33-2: Dante: He listens well who takes notes – from Italian: *Bene ascolta chi la nota.*

Rule 33-3: Churchill: Courage is what it takes to stand up and speak; courage is also what it takes to sit down and listen.

Rule 33-4: Napoleon: Never ascribe to malice that which is adequately explained by incompetence.

Japan, Kyoto (678, it was the imperial capital of Japan for over 1,000 years): Kyoto Central Post Office, north-west of Kyoto Railway Station.

34 - Exceptional Results

34 - **Advisers should have exceptional results obtained from their work, and based on these results, plus modesty, moderation, good character, friendliness, sharp mind, wisdom, good morals, and intense desire to help people, they will be elected, without any campaigning, publicity, fundraising, donations, debates, propaganda, political parties, advertising, or similar activities.**

Rule 34-1: It is highly recommended the use of advanced digital technology, which opens up entirely new opportunities for developing direct democracy, and public control institutions, improving the transparency of the election procedure, and taking into account the interests and opinions of each voter.

Rule 34-2: Voters are all people over the age of 21, who are not in a special medical institution for bad behavior or for mental health.

Rule 34-3: Polite dialogue and respect for everybody will be the norm.

Rule 34-4: Plato's recommendation will be applied: "Access to power must be confined to those who are not in love with it."

Rule 34-5: Otto von Bismarck: People never lie so much as before an election, during a war, or after a hunt.

Rule 34-6: Beethoven: This is the mark of a really admirable man: steadfastness in the face of trouble.

Rule 34-7: Stendhal: Only great minds can afford a simple style.

Rule 34-8: Thucydides: Ignorance is bold and knowledge reserved.

35 - Also Local Administrators

35 – <u>All Advisors should be also be local Administrators</u>.

Rule 35-1: All those interested in being Advisors should clearly know that *Either learn or leave* – from Latin: Aut disce aut discede.

France, Chamonix, entrance from France in Mont Blank tunnel (1959-1965, 11.6 km, 8.6 m by 4.35 m, elevation 1274 m) on 21 Oct 2015, 9:43 AM. The highway tunnel links Chamonix, Haute-Savoie, France with Courmayeur, Aosta Valley, Italy, via European route E25.

36 - Total and Complete Disarmament

36 – **For practical reasons, the transition from the current imperfect situation to the much better Sustainable Peace and Prosperity Structure (SPPS) will be very smooth: first - all the countries remain as they are, and they will begin – let's say on January 1st, 2020 - to negotiate total and complete disarmament, with the help of the United Nations. All the military units will become strong civilian organizations, working to improve the quality of life for everybody**.

Switzerland, Lausanne (Roman 150, 147,000, 41 km^2, 500 m elevation, 62 km northeast of Geneva, the home of the International Olympic Committee), near Château d'Ouchy (1170, 1609, 1893).

37 - Current Administrators

37 – **The current administrators (mayors, town managers, governors, etc.) will continue their work, and 20 months after - let's say January 1st, 2020 - will be – therefore on September 1st, 2022 - a quiet election – people will select new administrators from a short list of candidates, based on their written and verified qualifications.**

Rule 37-1: Jefferson: Whenever you do a thing, act as if the entire world were watching.

Rule 37-2: Horace: Make a good use of the present.

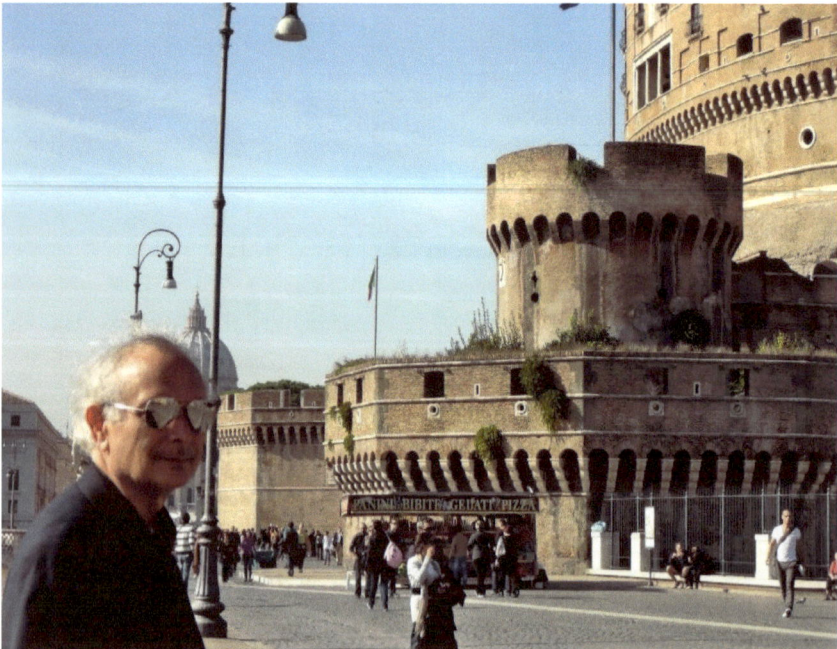

Rome (753 BC): from Lungotevere Prati, the south-east side of the Mausoleum (right, 135-139) of Hadrian (76–138, Emperor 117-138, renamed Castel Sant'Angelo in 600).

38 - Census

38 – **A census will take place every 5 years – starting, let's say on October 1st, 2023 - and all the people will receive a special credit card (SCC), with their photo and other personal data.**

Botticelli, 41, 1486, The Birth of Venus

39 - Special Credit Card (SCC)

39 – <u>The special credit card (SCC) will be used to buy everything, to identify for voting, for census, for travel, for medical assistance, etc. The current private credit cards will continue to work as usual.</u>

Rule 39-1: Aesop: No act of kindness, no matter how small, is ever wasted.
Slow and steady wins the race.
In union there is strength.
Gratitude is the sign of noble souls.

USA, Newport (1639): The southeast side of Isaac Bell (1846-1889, businessman and Ambassador to the Netherlands) House (Edna Villa), 1882, 4046 m².

40 - World Central Bank

40 – <u>The SCC will be issued by the World Central Bank, which will include all current central banks – starting, let's say on May 1st, 2023.</u>

Rule 40-1: Pliny the Elder: No mortal is wise at all times from Latin: *Nemo mortalium omnibus horis sapit.*

Rule 40-2: Benjamin Franklin: An investment in knowledge pays the best interest.

Switzerland, Geneva, on Quai du Mont Blanc, Beau Rivage Hotel (right, 1865, Mayer family, in 1918 Czechoslovakia creation document was signed here).

41 - Also Advisors

41 – <u>After one year - therefore on September 1st, 2023 - the newly elected administrators, based on quiet elections, will become also Advisors for the remaining 8 months, until April 30th, 2024, maintaining their administrative duties.</u>

Rule 41-1: Plato: He who is not a good servant will not be a good master.

USA, Boston (1630) Harbor, 11 July 2009, tall ships at Boston Fish Pier.

42 – Advisors Level

**42 – Advisors Level 1 (AL1) will be for 10,000 people,
AL2, elected as the best AL1 from 10 neighboring districts,
therefore for 100,000 people,
same for AL3 for 1,000,000,
AL4 for 10,000,000,
AL5 for 100,000,000,
and finally, the last 10 Advisors Level 6 (AL6) elected as the best
AL5 from the big 7 or 8 districts within those meridians
described at points 9 and 10, therefore for 770,000,000 people
each.**

Rule 42-1: All Advisors will have in mind:
Confucius: Do not impose on others, what you yourself do not desire.
Confucius: He acts before he speaks, and afterwards speaks according to his actions.
Descartes: It is not enough to have a good mind. The main thing is to use it well.
Cicero: Brevity is the best recommendation of speech.

Rule 42-2: Good achievers need reliable feedback from their teams; for this they cultivate an atmosphere of trust and collaboration.

Rule 42-3: Advisers need to provide what the people want, or even better.

Rule 42-4: Advisors need to know how to release the energy and talent of their teams.

Rule 42-5: Benjamin Franklin: Remember not only to say the right thing in the right place, but far more difficult still, to leave unsaid the wrong thing at the tempting moment.

Rule 42-6: Napoleon: Let the path be open to talent.

Italy, Milano: 30 Sep 2008, in Piazza del Duomo, looking southeast to the north side of il Duomo (Basilica cattedrale metropolitana di Santa Maria Nascente, 1386-1965 (579 years), capacity 40,000, length 158.5 m, width 92 m, maximum height 108 m, 135 spires, materials: brick and Candoglia marble, architects: Donato Bramante (1444-1514), Leonardo da Vinci (1452-1519), Giulio Romano (1499-1546), Pellegrino Tibaldi (1527-1596)). On May 20, 1805, Napoleon Bonaparte (1769-1821), about to be crowned King of Italy, ordered the façade to be finished by Pellicani. For this, a statue of Napoleon was placed at the top of one of the spires. Napoleon was crowned King of Italy at the Duomo on May 26, 1805.

43 - First Adviser for one Month, by Rotation

43 – **As mentioned at point 14, the top management will be formed of 10 Advisers Level 6, each of them will be the First Adviser for one month, by rotation.**
They will work by consensus only.
The First Adviser only coordinates the work of the other 9 Advisors for one month;
at the end of that month, the First Adviser will present in writing for the world (no more than 5 standard pages) a clear and precise Monthly World Report, with a list of finished and unfinished tasks;
the other 9 Advisers will add their comments to the Monthly World Report (no more than half a page each).
The top 10 Advisers will manage Police and all other Departments.
For obvious uncooperative or improper attitude of one top Advisor X, the other 9 can replace X with X's number 2.

Rule 43-1: The higher Advisors are placed, the more humbly they should be.

Rule 43-2: The pursuit of any activity ought to be calm and tranquil.

Rule 43-3: Achievement is not permanent success, but how fast you recover from a fiasco.

Rule 43-4: Good achievers know to divide difficult projects in manageable small tasks.

Rule 43-5: If you notice that you go in a wrong direction, the sooner you change the direction, the better.

Rule 43-6: If you work hard, in a good direction, with a clear and useful objective, the success will suddenly find you.

Rule 43-7: Logic and imagination go hand in hand for great achievers.

Rule 43-8: Some failures and errors are inevitable; use them to learn and improve.

Rule 43-9: Plato: The measure of a man is what he does with power.

Rule 43-10: After each Monthly World Report, a public opinion survey should be taken and presented to all Advisors.

Rule 43-11: All Advisors should be skeptic optimists.

Rule 43-12: Beethoven: Nothing is more intolerable than to have to admit to yourself your own errors.

Rule 43-13: Pasteur: It is surmounting difficulties that makes heroes.

Rule 43-14: Pasteur: Science knows no country, because knowledge belongs to humanity, and is the torch which illuminates the world.

Rule 43-15: Pasteur: There are no such things as applied sciences, only applications of science. It does not exist a category of science to which one can give the name applied science. There are science and the applications of science, bound together as the fruit of the tree which bears it.

Rule 43-16: Brahms: Without craftsmanship, inspiration is a mere reed shaken in the wind.

Rule 43-17: Much can be learned from accomplishments, but even more from fiascos.

Rule 43-18: Always the mediocrities, and their banalities, dominate. Always!

Rule 43-19: Confucius: Success depends upon previous preparation, and without such preparation there is sure to be failure.
The cautious seldom err.

44 – People can Always Change Advisors

44 – <u>People will always be able to change some Advisors, if they do not perform at the expected level – simply present a petition and count electronically how many people agree. If more than half of the people who voted for a certain Advisor X want to change X, then X will be changed with the number 2 for that district.</u>

Rule 44-1: **Sancta simplicitas** (Sacred simplicity)

Japan, Osaka (645 AD, the 3rd largest city in Japan, capital of Osaka Prefecture on the main island Honshu): detail of Toyosaki shrine (1772, with the Emperor Kotoku and others enshrined here).

45 - Vacancies

45 - **When vacancies happen for Advisors, the number 2 for those districts will fill the vacancies.**

Rule 45-1: Dediu: In order to gain wisdom, and therefore to be closer to happiness, "vitam mutaveris saepe in meliores actus" (change your life often for the better).

Japan, Tsukuba, 20 November 2008, photographs and computer presentations at the High Energy Accelerator Research Organization (KEK, 1997) in Tsukuba Science City (1962), in Ibaraki, 60 km north-east of Tokyo.

46 - Assistants

46 – Each Advisor, at all levels, should have 5 immediate assistants: a mathematician for finance and all other calculations, a medical doctor for keeping everybody healthy, calm, polite, friendly and optimist, a CEO for good management, an engineer for all practical projects, and a teacher for education, training and related areas.

Rule 46-1: Stendhal: Politics in a literary work, is like a gun shot in the middle of a concert, something vulgar, and however, something which is impossible to ignore.

Rule 46-2: Bismarck: Politics ruins the character.

Rule 46-3: Napoleon: In politics stupidity is not a handicap.

Rule 46-4: Thucydides: Few things are brought to a successful issue by impetuous desire, but most by calm and prudent forethought.

47 - Specialized Medical Institutions

47 – **All misunderstandings, disagreements or conflicts of any nature will be treated by medical personnel (with police help when strict necessary), until all is back to normal. No prisons are necessary, only specialized medical institutions (in simple cases, the places where the treated people live can be used, with the necessary limitations and surveillance).**

Rule 47-1: Seneca: Man is something sacred for man.

Rome (753 BC): the east side of Pons Aelius (Bridge of Hadrian, 134 AD, 18 m, 5 spans, renamed Ponte Sant'Angelo in 600), south of Mausoleum (135-139) of Hadrian (76–138, Emperor 117-138, renamed Castel Sant'Angelo in 600), with 10 statues of angels.

48 - Simple Administrative Disagreements

48 – **For simple administrative disagreements, an Administrator from another region will serve as mediator, together with a medical doctor, a mathematician, a CEO (and other specialists as needed), for solving the disagreements in a matter of minutes or hours (maximum 10 hours).**

Italy, 29 Sep 2008, Venezia (421), Piazza San Marco (1084) looking north, Torre dell'Orologio (1499, left back), Basilica di San Marco (1173, center back), .Palazzo Ducale (Doge's Palace, 1424, right).

49 – Collaboration Methods

49 – The top 10 Advisers (and all the others) will collaborate via e-mail, telephone, videoconferences, mail, or face to face, when needed, to produce practical results for all people, very fast.

Rule 49-1: Reagan: Mr. Gorbachev, tear down this wall!

USA, Boston: 11 July 2009, at the northwest end of Boston Fish Pier, northwest of the Exchange Conference Center (right) a Lexington Minutemen (armed volunteers ready to go in a minute) unit in 1776 uniforms.

50 - Disorderly Behavior

50 – <u>Advisors with disorderly behavior will be medically treated, and, when necessary, will be changed with their number 2.</u>

Rule 50-1: Darwin: The very essence of instinct is that it's followed independently of reason.

Chicago (1833): above entrance decorations of the Tribune Tower (1925, 36 floors, 141 m, for Chicago Tribune (1847)), with stones from famous places around the world, and from the Moon, including Harvard University, Arc de Triomph, Switzerland, Great Wall, Parthenon, Taj Mahal, Notre-Dame, and St. Peter's Basilica.

51 – Activities Recorded

51 – **All the activities of all Advisors will be recorded in computers and videos, and on paper, such that the people, who are interested, to be able to see what they are doing.**

Rule 51-1: Thomas Jefferson: Information is the currency of democracy.

Niagara Falls (8000 BC, the highest flow rate in the world), with the American Falls (left, USA, 21-30 m drop, 290 m wide), the Bridal Veil Falls (center, USA, 21 m drop, 10 m wide) and the Horseshoe Falls (center-right, in Canada, 53 m drop, 790 m wide).

52 – No Conflicts

52 – Because the objective is not to have any conflicts on Earth, the secrecy will slowly disappear.

Rule 52-1: Niels Bohr: The best weapon of a dictatorship is secrecy, but the best weapon of a democracy should be the weapon of openness.

Rule 52-2: The loudness and aggressiveness are invers proportional to the intelligence and reason.

Rule 52-3: Hoover: Older men declare war. But it is youth that must fight and die.

Rule 52-4: Hoover: Peace is not made at the council table or by treaties, but in the hearts of men.

Rule 52-5: Churchill: If the human race wishes to have a prolonged and indefinite period of material prosperity, they have only got to behave in a peaceful and helpful way toward one another.
If we open a quarrel between past and present, we shall find that we have lost the future.
If you go on with this nuclear arms race, all you are going to do is make the rubble bounce.
If you have ten thousand regulations you destroy all respect for the law.

Rule 52-6: The conflicts must be stopped **Seculo seculorum** (Forever and ever).

Rule 52-7: Edison: Non-violence leads to the highest ethics, which is the goal of all evolution.

London, Parliament Square, the bronze statue (1973) of Sir Winston Churchill (1874-1965, Prime Minister 1940-1945, 1951-1955 (as Prime Minister he lived at 10 Downing Street, just 400 m northwest (right) from this place; as Churchill's youngest daughter, Mary Soames (1922-2014) had the run of 10 Downing Street, and helped arrange dinner with Stalin (1878-1953) in Moscow, 1942), created by the British sculptor Ivor Roberts-Jones (1913-1996).

53 - 40 hours/week

53 – **Advisors at all levels should work 40 hours/week, with 4 weeks vacation, but many services (medical, police (firemen should be part of the police), volunteers) should be non-stop.**

Rule 53-1: Seneca: Luck is what happens when preparation meets opportunity.

Italy, 23 October 2009, Trieste (177 BC part of the Roman Republic), from Passo Fausto Pecorari, in Piazza San Giovanni, looking southeast to the statue of Giuseppe Verdi (1813-1901), and buildings on Via Giacinto Gallina (left) and Via delle Torri (right).

54 - Compensation

54 – <u>Advisors' compensation should be the world annual average salary (in 2019 less than $10,000) plus 6% of that world average salary, for level 6 (total $10,600), + 5 % for level 5, and so on. They all should work to increase the world average salary, in order to get themselves an increase.</u>

Rule 54-1: Euler: Nothing at all takes place in the universe in which some rule of maximum or minimum does not appear.

Rule 54-2: Stendhal: Pleasure is often spoiled by describing it.

Rule 54-3: Edison: What a man's mind can create, man's character can control.

Japan, 24 Nov 2008, inside Hyogo Earthquake Engineering Center, the biggest earthquake research center in the world, in Miki City, near Kobe. Buildings tested on the Earthquake Defense shake table.

55 - Honorific World Observer

55 – <u>A Honorific World Observer should be quietly elected by direct vote – starting, let's say September 1st, 2022 - for only one 3 years term, with the request to observe that the top 10 Advisers efficiently perform their duties, and keep their words – if they don't, they must be changed.</u>

Rule 55-1: Rousseau: Falsehood has an infinity of combinations, but truth has only one mode of being.

Rule 55-2: Kant: By a lie, a man... annihilates his dignity as a man.

Rule 55-3: Kant: Ingratitude is the essence of vileness.

Rule 55-4: Stendhal: The shepherd always tries to persuade the sheep that their interests and his own are the same.

Rule 55-5: Rousseau: Force does not constitute right... obedience is due only to legitimate powers.
Insults are the arguments employed by those who are in the wrong.
Man was born free, and he is everywhere in chains.
No man has any natural authority over his fellow men.

56 - Free to Speak

56 – <u>All Advisors are free to speak about their administrative work, with modesty.</u>

Rule 56-1: Virgil: Mind drives matter - from Latin: ***Mens agitat molem.***

Rule 56-2: Arrogance and self-importance are everywhere, modesty is a rara avis (rare bird).

UK, London, From the Westminster Bridge (1862) looking southwest to the Palace of Westminster (1016, 1870), Big Ben (1855, 96 m, right).

57 – Tax: 15% of income

57 – **The tax will be 15% for everybody in the world.**

Italy, Rome: Accademia Nazionale dei Lincei (1603) in Villa Farnesina (1510). The author was invited to give a lecture here in 1978.

58 - Savings Accounts for Old Age

58 – **Everybody should have a savings account for old age (the old age will be starting around 70), and 10% of their income should automatically go to their savings accounts. For those unable to work, their doctors and mathematicians will decide case by case. All families will assist their parents, grandparents, and great-grandparents.**

Japan, 21 November 2008, Kawaguchiko, looking south to the north side of Mount Fuji (3,776 m, 1707 last eruption) seen from 17 km north.

59 - All budgets will have 2% surplus

59 – <u>All the budgets, at all levels, will have a 2% surplus, which will be returned to the taxpayers.</u>

Rule 59-1: Horace: It is easy to be generous with things of another person – from Latin: facile largire de alieno. (It is well known that now all the governments take money from some people, and give it to others.)

Rule 59-2: Let not your spending exceed your income – from Latin: Sumptus censum ne superset.

Rule 59-3: Michelangelo: The greater danger for most of us lies not in setting our aim too high and falling short; but in setting our aim too low, and achieving our mark.

Rule 59-4: Reagan: No government ever voluntarily reduces itself in size. Government programs, once launched, never disappear. Actually, a government bureau is the nearest thing to eternal life we'll ever see on this earth!

Italy, Rome (753 BC): la Chiesa Parrochiale del Sacro Cuore del Suffragio (1894 – 1917, by Giuseppe Gualandi) on Lungotevere Prati, 50 m east of the Corte Suprema di Cassazione in Palazzo di Giustizia (1888 – 1911).

60 - Spending Proposals

60 – <u>All spending proposals from Advisers must be approved by their 5 assistants (doctors, mathematicians, CEOs, engineers and teachers), and must have an already existing funding in the budget.</u>

Rule 60-1: And always Sequere pecuniam - Follow the money.

Rule 60-2: Thrift is a great priority for all Advisors.

Rule 60-3: Cicero: It is not by muscle, speed, or physical dexterity that great things are achieved, but by reflection, force of character, and judgment.

Rule 60-4: Cato the Elder: Even though work stops, expenses run on.

Rule 60-5: Sophocles: To be doing good deeds is man's most glorious task.
Success is dependent on effort.
Who seeks shall find.
Without labor nothing prospers.
Fortune cannot aid those who do nothing.
Our happiness depends on wisdom all the way.

61 - 7 Small Departments

61 – The World Government should be limited to 7 small departments: Tax Department, Treasury, People Assistance Department, Medical Department, Police, Education Department, Science & Technology Department.

Rule 61-1: Virgil: It is imperative to be well trained in early youth – from Latin: *Adeo in teneris consuescere multum est.*

Rule 61-2: Virgil: From one example, learn all – from Latin: *Ab uno disce omnes.*

Rule 61-3: Galileo Galilei: In questions of science, the authority of a thousand is not worth the humble reasoning of a single individual.

Rule 61-4: Galileo Galilei: Mathematics is the language with which God has written the universe.

Rule 61-5: Galileo Galilei: The Sun, with all those planets revolving around it and dependent upon it, can still ripen a bunch of grapes as if it had nothing else in the universe to do.

62 – No borrowing

62 – **Advisers cannot borrow money.**

Rule 62-1: Washington: Worry is the interest paid by those who borrow trouble.

USA, Boston, 20 June 2015, Boston Public Garden (1837), statue of George Washington (1732-1799), by Thomas Ball in 1869.

63 - Rules Proposed by Advisers

63 - **All rules proposed by Advisers must be approved by their 5 assistants (doctors, mathematicians, CEOs, engineers and teachers), and for any new rule over 2,000 basic rules (each rule on at most half a page, total 1,000 pages), at least on old rule must be eliminated.**

Rule 63-1: Augustus: Make haste slowly – from Latin: *Festina lente.*

Japan, Kobe (201 AD, the 5th largest city in Japan, 30 km west of Osaka): a delightful Academy Bar, since 1922.

64 - Remain in Their Places

64 – **All people in the world will remain in their places, and the improvements will come to them. Those who want to move to other places, will need first a special invitation from at least 10 people (not family related) where they want to move.**

Rule 64-1: Cicero: To stumble twice against the same stone is a proverbial disgrace.

Rome (753 BC), Vatican (1929): Piazza di San Pietro (1656 – 1667, Bernini), with Moderno's façade (115 m wide, 46 m high) of the Basilica di San Pietro (1506 – 1626), and an Egyptian obelisk.

65 – Bankruptcies

65 – Bankruptcies, in general, will be discouraged, and when strict necessary, will be analyzed and solved, case by case, by the doctors, mathematicians and CEOs who worked with the people who asked the bankruptcy.

Rule 65-1: It is important to have in mind that *To err is human, to persevere is of the devil* – from Latin: Errare humanum est, perseverare diabolicum.

Rule 65-2: Edison: There is no substitute for hard work.

Rule 65-3: Edison: Just because something doesn't do what you planned it to do, doesn't mean it's useless.

Rule 65-4: Edison: Nearly every man, who develops an idea, works it up to the point where it looks impossible, and then he gets discouraged. That's not the place to become discouraged.

Rule 65-5: Edison: Opportunity is missed by most people because it is dressed in overalls and looks like work.

Rule 65-6: Edison: The best thinking has been done in solitude. The worst has been done in turmoil.

Rule 65-7: Edison: The three great essentials to achieve anything worthwhile are: Hard work, Stick-to-itiveness, and Common sense.

Rule 65-8: When somebody X is making a mistake, everybody around X should interrupt X, and help X to correct the mistake.

Rule 65-9: Darwin: A man, who dares to waste one hour of time, has not discovered the value of life.

Italy, Udine: 3 November 2009, on the northwest side of Piazza della Liberta, looking southeast to il Torre dell'Orologio (1527, left), Porticato di San Giovanni (1533, center left), Via Vittorio Veneto (center right down), il Campanile della Chiesa del Duomo (center right up), the column (1539) with San Marco's lion (the symbol of Venezia (la Serenissima), right).

66 - New World Currency

66 – **Advisors should create a new world currency, named, let's say "coin", and all the other currencies will be exchanged for coins.**

USA, Bretton Woods: The Gold Room in the Mount Washington Resort, where the documents of the United Nations Monetary and Financial Conference were signed in July 1944.

67 - International Standards

67 - The Standard of Weights and Measures will be the current International Standards.

France, Paris: Mannequins representing Gustave Eiffel (right, 57 years old) talking in 1889 to Thomas Edison (left, 42 years old) in Eiffel's apartment in Tour Eiffel (1889, 324 m).

On Gagarin (First Man in Space) Terrace, on the southwest part of the South Building (1899) of the Royal Observatory Greenwich (1676), looking northeast to the south part of the west side (right), the west part of the south side (left), and to the statue of Yuri Gagarin (1934-1968, aged 34, Russian cosmonaut, the first man in space, with Vostok, which completed an orbit (1h 48') of the Earth on 12 April 1961, at age 27. Resting place: Kremlin Wall Necropolis).

68 – If Bad - Pay All Expense and Reimburse

68 – **The counterfeiting and all other bad things, which some sick people do, will be medically treated (in specialized medical institutions when necessary), and those who did bad things will pay all the expenses, and will reimburse the victims. Victims will always be very protected, and helped to recover the losses from the attackers.**

Rule 68-1: Plato: Justice in the life and conduct of the State is possible only as first it resides in the hearts and souls of the citizens.

Rule 68-2: Plato: No law or ordinance is mightier than understanding.

Rule 68-3: Plato: The highest reach of injustice is to be deemed just when you are not.

Rule 68-4: Darwin: To kill an error is as good a service as, and sometimes even better than, the establishing of a new truth or fact.

69 - World Post Offices, Intellectual Rights

69 – World Post Offices will include the current ones, which will be interconnected, improved and modernized.
- The intellectual rights will be respected, based mostly on the current rules, managed by assistants.

Japan, Inzai: 19 November 2008, on a street 350 m northeast of the Inzai campus of Tokyo Denki University (1907, 1949), looking northeast to the Inzai Post Office (right).

70 - People Assistance Services

70 – <u>All the Tribunals and related areas will be transformed in people assistance services, based on friendliness, collaboration and goodwill.</u>

Rule 70-1: These people assistance services will always act thinking first *Do to another as you do to yourself* – from Latin: Alteri sic tibi.

Rule 70-2: Herodotus: To think well, and to consent to obey someone giving good advice, are the same thing.

Rule 70-3: Sophocles: Always desire to learn something useful.

Rule 70-4: Virgil: - Fortunate is he, who understood the causes of things – from Latin: Felix, qui potuit rerum cognoscere causas.

Rule 70-5: Shakespeare: Love all, trust a few, do wrong to none.

Rule 70-6: Shakespeare: Better three hours too soon than a minute too late.

Rule 70-7: Darwin: The highest possible stage in moral culture is when we recognize that we ought to control our thoughts.

Rule 70-8: Good instincts are fine, but bad instincts must be medically corrected.

Rule 70-9: Edison: There is no expedient to which a man will not go to avoid the labor of thinking.

Rule 70-10: Edison: What you are, will show in what you do.

Rule 70-11: Edison: It is astonishing what an effort it seems to be for many people to put their brains definitely and systematically to work.

Rule 70-12: Whitehead: Civilizations can only be understood by those who are civilized.

Rule 70-13: Hoover: About the time we can make the ends meet, somebody moves the ends.

Rule 70-14: Democritus: Good means not merely not to do wrong, but rather not to desire to do wrong.

Rule 70-15: Seneca: One of the most beautiful qualities of true friendship is to understand and to be understood.

Rule 70-16: Seneca: Wherever there is a human being, there is an opportunity for a kindness.

Rule 70-17: In some cases, like children, elderly, or disable people, the assistance personnel should not wait for their requests for help. The assistance personnel must attend to everyone, find out what they need, help fill in the necessary documents and papers (or do it for them, if necessary), support, submit the documents where necessary and, most importantly, control all this and make sure that the work is done. Do not just forget about these papers, but see this through. Everyone will do something useful and improve the world, rather than waste time in litigation.

Japan, Tokyo (1180), special ward Shinjuku, from the 45th fl., 202 m, of Tokyo Met. Gov Bldg. North Tower): Shinjuku Sumitomo Bldg. (210 m, 52 fl, 1974, center), Shinjuku Mitsui Building (224 m, 55 floors, 1974, right).

71 - Oceans

71 – **All the oceans will belong to some of the regions defined at point 9, therefore will be maintained by those regions, to be free of any piracy or other bad activity – World Police will help when necessary.**

Rule 71-1: Ovid: All things change, nothing perishes – from Latin: *Omnia mutantur, nihil interit.*

Australia: In Sydney (1788, 5 M people), from the Royal Botanic Gardens looking northwest to the southeast side of the harbourfront Sydney Opera House (1959-1973, 183 m by 120 m by 65 m height, total seating capacity 5738)) and the Sydney Harbour Bridge (1932, left).

Constanta, Romania, Piazza Ovidiu: Statue of Publius Ovidius Naso (20 March 43 BC, in Sulmona – 17, in Tomis, Moesia (now Constanta, Romania), aged circa 59, close to the place where Ovidius died.

72 – No War

72 – **Advisors (and all the others) cannot declare war, reprisals or capture land or water.**

Rule 72-1: War existed always, and the history is just a succession of wars, but now, finally, most people understand that the time has arrived to switch from eternal wars and preparing for wars, to eternal peace and preparing for happiness! This is the key idea for which everybody will work.

Rule 72-2: Adversity will disappear, and peace, freedom and prosperity will flourish, because *Life is not being alive, but being well* – from Latin: Vita non est vivere, sed valere vita est.

Rule 72-3: There is a good precedent: Calvin Coolidge (age 56.1), the 30th U. S. President - "It is accordance with our determination to refrain from aggression and build up a sentiment and practice among nations more favorable to peace…that we have incurred the consent of fourteen important nations to the negotiations of a treaty condemning recourse to war, renouncing it as an instrument of national policy." Calvin Coolidge (1872-1933), U.S president. New York Times (August 16, 1928)
This refers to the Kellogg–Briand Pact (or Pact of Paris, officially General Treaty for Renunciation of War as an Instrument of National Policy), which is a 1928 international agreement in which signatory states promised not to use war to resolve "disputes or conflicts of whatever nature or of whatever origin they may be, which may arise among them". Parties failing to abide by this promise "should be denied of the benefits furnished by [the] treaty". It was signed by Germany, France, and the United States on 27 August 1928, and by most other states (total of 62) soon after. Sponsored by France and the U.S., the Pact renounced the use of war and calls for the peaceful settlement of disputes. Similar provisions were incorporated into the Charter of the United Nations and other treaties. It is named after its authors, United States

Secretary of State, Frank B. Kellogg, and French foreign minister, Aristide Briand. The pact was concluded outside the League of Nations, came into effect on 24 July 1929, and remains in effect. With the signing of the Litvinov Protocol in Moscow on February 9, 1929, the Soviet Union and its western neighbors, including Romania, agreed to put the Kellogg-Briand Pact in effect, without waiting for other western signatories to ratify. The Bessarabian Question (the eastern part of the Romanian northeastern province Moldova) had made agreement between Romania and the Soviet Union challenging, and dispute between the nations over Bessarabia continued until 1939, when the Soviet Union occupied by force Bessarabia, which remains in effect. Now we just enlarge and improve this good beginning, solving all remaining disputes and historical errors.

Rule 72-4: Plato: When the tyrant has disposed of foreign enemies by conquest or treaty, and there is nothing more to fear from them, then he is always stirring up some war or other, in order that the people may require a leader.

Rule 72-5: Aeschylus: In war, truth is the first casualty.

Rule 72-6: Aeschylus: Everyone's quick to blame the alien.

Rule 72-7: Edison: There will one day spring from the brain of science a machine or force so fearful in its potentialities, so absolutely terrifying, that even man, the fighter, who will dare torture and death in order to inflict torture and death, will be appalled, and so abandon war forever.

73 – No Military Forces

73 – **Advisors (and all the others) cannot raise and support armies, navy, or any military forces.**

Rule 73-1: The new aphorism is: If you want peace, prepare for peace.

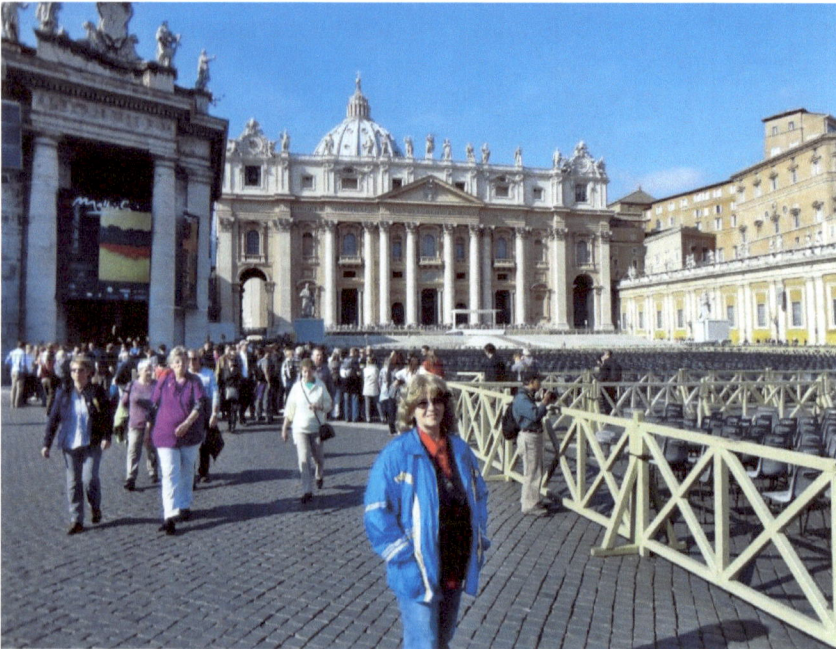

Rome (753 BC), Vatican (1929): Piazza di San Pietro (1656 – 1667, Bernini) with Moderno's façade (115 m wide, 46 m high) of the Basilica di San Pietro (1506 – 1626), with 13 statues. Christ, 11 of the Apostles and John the Baptist.

74 – Some Police with Small Arms

74 – **Police will be the only department which will have some small arms, in order to stop some very bad people (who are very sick).**

Australia: Sydney Monorail (1988, closed after 25 years in 2013, 3.6 km, connected Darling Harbour (in photo), Chinatown and the Sydney central business and shopping districts, 8 stations, 6 trains).

75 - Police Will Work with Others

75 – **Police will work with medical personnel, mathematicians, CEOs, engineers, teachers and others, to make sure that all the people on the Planet are in good mental health, in order to prevent bad situations. This is also a major responsibility of all Advisors.**

Rule 75-1: Conflict resolution will be dome only through negotiation and mediation.

Rule 75-2: Entrepreneurial negotiation will be supported and applied.

Rule 75-3: Vegetius: Few men are born brave. Many become so through training and force of discipline.

In Malmö, southwest of Sweden, taking the boat from Malmö to Köpenhamn (Copenhagen, Denmark, 25 km northwest of Malmö).

76 - Budget for Police

76 – **The Advisors will allocate the necessary budget for Police, and Police will assist people in need.**

France, Paris: In the main courtyard of the Musée du Louvre (1793, the world's largest museum, historic palace (1180), on the right bank of la Seine), with the glass pyramid (1989, 21 m, for the entranceway, left).

77 - Government Buildings

77 – <u>The Advisors will be located in the current government buildings, and the excess government buildings and properties will be sold, in order to increase the budget and to reduce the expenses.</u>

Sweden, Malmö, from Skeppsbron looking north to the north part of the west side of the Central Station (right), sign for Trelleborg and Limhamn (to left), Goteborg and Hamnen (straight).

Japan, Tokyo (1180), special ward Shinjuku: Tokyo Metropolitan Government Building, 243 m, 48 floors, 1991, with two observation decks on floor 45, at 202 m.

78 - Common Sense

78 – <u>Not many rules will be necessary, because the people will be more civilized and friendly, and the common sense (ad iudicium) will be the main rule.</u>

Rule 78-1: Plato: To prefer evil to good is not in the human nature; and when a man is compelled to choose one of two evils, no one will choose the greater when he might have the less.

Rule 78-2: Pythagoras: Silence is better than unmeaning words.

Rule 78-3: Michelangelo: There is no greater harm than that of time wasted.

Rule 78-4: Galileo Galilei: I do not feel obliged to believe that the same God, who has endowed us with sense, reason, and intellect, has intended us to forgo their use.

Rule 78-5: Descartes: Nothing is more fairly distributed than common sense: no one thinks he needs more of it than he already has.

Rule 78-6: Voltaire: Common sense is not so common.

Rule 78-7: Whitehead: Common sense is genius in homespun.

79 – Free Commerce

79 – The commerce between the people on the Earth should be free of taxes, tariffs, duties, etc.

Michelangelo, 36, completed The Creation of Man (1510-1511), a fresco on the vault of the Sistine Chapel. The Lord's gesture is superb, as His mighty arm becomes the channel for the life force. Adam's arm resting passively on his knee. These two figures are the best known of all Sistine paintings.

80 – Government Website

80 – **Again, all the activity of the Advisors, and others from the small World Government, should be available to the people on a website.**

Rule 80-1: People will always ask the small World Government *Deeds, not words* – from Latin: Facta non verba.

France, Paris: On a boat sur la Seine, looking upstream, northeast, to the left bank (right): Port de Grenelle (right), near Quai de Grenelle, the southwest side of la Tour Eiffel (1889, 324 m), Île aux Cygnes (left), a bridge for railroad, and after it Pont de Bir-Hakeim (1905).

81 - Nobility

81 – <u>Nobility (King, Prince, etc.) could continue to exist in some places, but they should not interfere with activities of the Advisors, and actually should help them.</u>

Rule 81-1: Washington: I hope I shall possess firmness and virtue enough to maintain what I consider the most enviable of all titles, the character of an honest man.

London's only planetarium bronze cone (the largest in the world, 250 welded plates). The cone is sliced at angle parallel to celestial equator, the line on the slice is north (left, perpendicular) south (up) is parallel to 0 meridian, angle of the southern side (right) is equal to the latitude of Royal Observatory Greenwich 51° 22' 44" N.

82 – Changing Rules

82 – <u>All the rules can be changed or eliminated when a majority of the people or their Advisors agree, but some fundamental peace and order rules will remain.</u>

Rule 82-1: Cicero: The more laws, the less justice.

Rule 82-2: Cicero: What is permissible is not always honorable.

Australia, Sydney: From the south of the Sydney Opera House, looking north to a restaurant (left) and the south side of the Opera (center and right).

83 - Religion

83 – <u>The religion should be free, and is expected not to interfere with activities of the Advisors, and actually should help people.</u>

France, Paris: L'Église de la Madeleine (or L'Église Sainte-Marie-Madeleine, or La Madeleine, 1842), a Roman Catholic Church in the 8th arrondissement of Paris, designed by Napoleon in 1806.

84 – No Abuses

84 – **Special attention will be given by Advisors to avoid abuses and wrong interpretations of the rules. All assistants (doctors, mathematicians, CEOs, engineers and teachers) will closely monitor all activities, to avoid abuses and wrong interpretations of the rules.**

Japan, Osaka, ladies in kimono (means thing to wear, now it is very formal and polite clothing, generally worn with traditional footwear (zori or geta) and with split-toe socks (tabi)).

85 – Speech Free and Responsible

85 – <u>The speech should be free, and is expected not to call for war, violence, or similar destructive activities. People want peace, freedom, health, friendship and prosperity.</u>

Rule 85-1: Remember Churchill: A lie gets halfway around the world before the truth has a chance to get its pants on.

Rule 85-1: Epictetus: Only the educated are free.

Rule 85-2: Cicero: Brevity is a great charm of eloquence.

Rule 85-3: Cicero: One should employ restraint in his jests – from Latin: ***Adhibenda est in iocando moderatio.***

Rule 85-4: Shakespeare: Brevity is the soul of wit.

Rule 85-5: Jefferson: All tyranny needs to gain a foothold is for people of good conscience to remain silent.

Rule 85-6: Jefferson: An association of men, who will not quarrel with one another, is a thing which has never yet existed, from the greatest confederacy of nations, down to a town meeting or a vestry.

Rule 85-6: Jefferson: When angry count to ten before you speak. If very angry, count to one hundred.

Rule 85-7: Mozart: My great-grandfather used to say to his wife, my great-grandmother, who in turn told her daughter, my grandmother, who repeated it to her daughter, my mother, who used to remind her daughter, my own sister, that to talk well and eloquently is a very great art, but that an equally great one is to know the right moment to stop.

Rule 85-8: Lincoln: Better to remain silent and be thought a fool, than to speak out and remove all doubt.

Rule 85-9: Churchill: Broadly speaking, the short words are the best, and the old words best of all.

Rule 85-10: Hoover: It is a paradox that every dictator has climbed to power on the ladder of free speech. Immediately on attaining power each dictator has suppressed all free speech except his own.

Rule 85-11: Herodotus: It is clear that not in one thing alone, but in many ways, equality and freedom of speech are a good thing.

USA, California, Berkeley, in a beautiful garden near Claremont Sport.

Japan, Kyoto (678, it was the imperial capital of Japan for over 1,000 years): Kyoto Tower Hotel, on Shiokoji Dori, 200 m north of Kyoto Railway Station.

86 - The press Should Be Free and Responsible

86 – **The press should be free, and is expected not to call for war, violence, or similar destructive activities. People want peace, freedom, health, friendship and prosperity.**

Rule 86-1: Plato: Excess of liberty, whether it lies in state or individuals, seems only to pass into excess of slavery.

Rule 86-2: Plato: Without effort, you cannot be prosperous. Though the land be good, you cannot have an abundant crop without cultivation.

USA, Worcester: 23 Jan 2010, looking east to the central entrance on the southern façade of the Boynton Hall, WPI, 1865.

87 – People Can Assemble Peacefully Only

87 – **People can assemble peacefully only, with police for help, and is expected not to call for war, violence, or similar destructive activities. People want peace, freedom, health, friendship and prosperity.**

Rule 87-1: Thucydides: Be convinced that to be happy means to be free, and that to be free means to be brave.

Rule 87-2: Stendhal: To describe happiness is to diminish it.

Rule 87-3: J. S. Mill: I have learned to seek my happiness by limiting my desires, rather than in attempting to satisfy them.

Rule 87-4: J. S. Mill: Unquestionably, it is possible to do without happiness; it is done involuntarily by nineteen-twentieths of mankind.

88 – People Can Petition the Word Government

88 – **People of course can petition the small Word Government, and can change it anytime, if it does not perform as expected.**

Rule 88-1: People are encouraged to inform the small Word Government about abuses, corruption, immorality and other vices, otherwise *A vice is nourished by being concealed* (from Latin: Alitur vitium vivitque tegendo).

Rule 88-2: The small Word Government should quickly adapt to changes, because *All things change, and we change with them* – from Latin: Omnia mutantur nos et mutamur in illis.

Rule 88-3: Leonardo da Vinci: Nothing strengthens authority so much as silence.

Rule 88-4: J. S. Mill: A person may cause evil to others not only by his actions but by his inaction, and in either case he is justly accountable to them for the injury.

Rule 88-5: Darwin: It is not the strongest of the species that survive, nor the most intelligent, but the one most responsive to change.

Rule 88-6: Edison: Discontent is the first necessity of progress.

Rule 88-7: Voltaire: It is dangerous to be right when the government is wrong.

89 – Arms will Not Exist Anymore

89 – **Arms will not exist anymore, and only the police will have some small arms. Those who want arms for hunting or sport, will borrow them from police stations, with proper documents, rules and payments.**

Rule 89-1: All arms and military related industries will change to civilian production, so much needed in the world.

Rule 89-2: All arms and military equipment will be adapted for civilian use, when possible, or destroyed.

Italy, 8 Sep 1977, Sophia Dediu (34) at Cortona (20 km southeast of Arezzo (circa 1500 BC, 343 km^2, elevation 494 m, population 23,000)), the southwest façade and entrance of Il Palazzone di Cortona (1521-1527, 2 km southeast of Cortona).

90 - The Police Powers will be Limited

90 - **The police powers will be limited, and they will know and be friend with all the people in their jurisdiction – this is the key element of a civilized and peaceful Earth. If they notice a person with bad intentions, they immediately retain that person and call for a medical assistant (and other assistants, if necessary), to analyze and solve the issue.**

Rule 90-1: Police will be people's friend everywhere, and they will always help people.

Rule 90-2: Cicero: Friendship improves happiness and abates misery, by the doubling of our joy and the dividing of our grief.

Finland, Helsinki: 9 May 2013, tram 6 Hietalaati Sanoviken (trams first appeared in 1807 in the UK).

91 – Prevention of Bad Events

91 – **Prevention of bad events is the main objective of everybody. If a bad event occurs, the police and their assistants will eliminate the consequences, reestablish the normal situation, and determine why the bad event occurred, in order to improve their activity and prevent such bad events in the future.**

Rule 91-1: Very much effort and energy will be devoted to prevention of bad events, because prevention is much cheaper and healthier than the consequences of a bad event.

USA, Boston, 3 Dec 2009, from Avenue Louis Pasteur (1822-1895, French microbiologist), Boston Public Latin School (1635, Schola Latina Bostoniensis, the oldest and the first public exam school in the US).

92 - Nothing is Perfect

92 – **We know that nothing is perfect, but we must try hard to be as close as possible to perfection (not an easy job, of course, but it is doable, pleasant, and very useful)**.

Rule 92-1: Plato: Those who intend on becoming great should love neither themselves nor their own things, but only what is just, whether it happens to be done by themselves or others.

Rule 92-2: History is full of imperfections, and everybody must make sure that they are not repeated.

Rule 92-3: Stendhal: The first qualification for a historian is to have no ability to invent.

93 - Life, Liberty, or Property

93 – **A person cannot be deprived of life, liberty, or property, without having several doctors and other assistants agree: for life – at least 12; for liberty – at least 6; for property – at least 3. Also, a person cannot deprive another person of life, liberty, or property, which, unfortunately, occurs very frequently in the world, and very much effort and energy will be allocated to prevent such bad events.**

Rule 93-1: This is a major area of concern, and Advisors must work really hard to fast improve the world situation.

Slovenia, Ljubljana, 2 Nov 2009, statue of France Preseren (1800-1849, educated at the University of Vienna, the greatest Slovene poet), at Cyril and Methodius Square, in Ljubljana (80 km northeast of Trieste).

94 - Private property

94 - <u>Private property cannot be taken for public use, without just compensation, decided by at least 5 assistants</u>.

Rule 94-1: Unfortunately, many people in the world do not have any private property to warry about, but they will have, and then it will be protected.

Romania, Brasov (Kronstadt): 12 Oct 2008, From Capitol Hotel, looking northeast to the Town Hall, with Piata Tricolorului and Bulevardul Eroilor (down).

95 – When Somebody Does a Bad Thing

95 – **If a person X is considered that did a bad thing, X will have, within 3 days, a discussion with one or more doctors and other assistants, and will be informed of the nature and cause of the bad thing; including witnesses against and for him. Then a decision will be taken within other 3 days, by a group of doctors and other assistants. Victims of bad people will always have priority to discuss their problems with one or more doctors and other assistants, and quick decisions will be taken within 3 days, by a group of doctors and other assistants. Protection of victims has always priority.**

Rule 95-1: Advisors will work hard to protect victims against bad people – these bad people are sick and need medical attention.

Rule 95-2: Unfortunately, there is sometimes adversity in the world, but everybody should say "I repel adversity by valor" – from Latin "Adversa virtute repello".

96 - Simple Disputes

96 – **In very simple disputes or culpa levis (ordinary negligence, like late payments, etc.), one single assistant will decide within minutes, and all people will go back to work.**

Rule 96-1: **People want peace, freedom, health, friendship and prosperity, therefore disputes should be quickly resolved and then transformed in friendships.**

USA, Cambridge: 1 Feb 2010, on Massachusetts Avenue, looking northeast to the west façade of the Department of Urban Studies and Planning (left), and the main entrance to the MIT (1861, center).

97 – Special Attention to Victims

97 – **It is well understood that no excessive bail will be required, no excessive fines imposed, no cruel and unusual punishments applied, but, at the same time, it is well understood that a person who did a bad thing will receive the necessary corrective medical treatment, and will reimburse all people who suffered damages, and the medical treatment. The victims will always receive special attention.**

Rule 97-1: **People want peace, freedom, health, friendship and prosperity, therefore conflicts should be quickly resolved and then the corrective medical treatment will include the transformation of hostility and aggressiveness into harmony and friendship.**

Japan, Osaka, 25 Nov 2008, looking northwest to the main entrance of Toyosaki shrine (1772, with the Emperor Kotoku and others enshrined here, 300 m south of Yodo River, 100 m east of the freeway 423).

98 – Prevention First

98 – **<u>Again, in order to prevent bad things, the police, doctors and their assistants will be in permanent contact with all the people, by visiting them, phone calls, e-mails, videos, and mail, to keep everybody calm and happy.</u>**

Rule 98-1: Especially doctors and their assistants will give high attention to have everybody calm, peaceful and optimist.

Romania, Sibiu (Hermannstadt): 11 Oct 2008, in the Small Square, looking northwest to the Liars Bridge (1859, the first footbridge in Romania to have been cast in iron, its name comes from stories and tall talk of the nearby hagglers selling fish, center), and a bride being photographed (down).

99 – Language and Alphabet

99 – <u>For obvious reasons, it is very desirable to have a common language and alphabet on Earth. Because English is a de facto common language now, it would be desirable to take it as the basis of the world language, let's call it Mundo, which will be taught in all schools. All the other languages will continue as secondary languages. The same is true for the Latin alphabet, which will be used everywhere, with other alphabets as secondary.</u>

Rule 99-1: This is a laborious and important work, and especially teachers will have a very significant role.

Rule 99-2: Arthur Schopenhauer: Without books the development of civilization would have been impossible. They are the engines of change, windows on the world, "Lighthouses" as the poet said "erected in the sea of time." They are companions, teachers, magicians, bankers of the treasures of the mind. Books are humanity in print.

100 – Conclusions

100 – Conclusions:

- Rule 100-1: **Work for everybody: when somebody X is unemployed, X can ask for a temporary world minimum wage ($2/hour) job (assisting other people, for example), until finds a better job.**

- Rule 100-2: **To start this new structure, the first Honorific World Observer (from UN, for example) could invite 10 Presidents form big countries (like USA, China, Russia, UK, India, France, Japan, Germany, Brasil, and Egypt) to be the first 10 Advisors Level 6, starting, let's say on January 1st, 2020, for 10 months, until November 1st, 2020, when the new calm and noiseless elections will take place. The same for the 100 Advisers Level 5, and so on.**

- Rule 100-3: "Any man may easily do harm, but not every man can do good to another." Plato

- Rule 100-4: "Excess generally causes reaction, and produces a change in the opposite direction, whether it be in the seasons, or in individuals, or in governments." Plato

- Rule 100 – 5: 10 world holidays: the normal 4 Earth events (2 solstices and 2 equinoxes), Mother's Day on 1st May, Father's Day on 6 August, Children's Day on 6 November, Grandparents' Day on 6 February, and 2 optional days (like Thanksgiving or Religious Day (Christmas), and Earth or Future Day).

- Rule 100 – 6: In implementing this new good structure, everybody should say: I'll either find a way, or make one – From Latin: Aut viam inveniam, aut faciam.

Rule 100-7: Horace: If you can better these principles, tell me; if not, join me in following them. – From Latin: Si quid novisti rectius istis, candidus imperti; si nil, his utere mecum.

Rule 100-8: This sustainable peace, liberty, health, friendship and prosperity can be done and it will be done – the sooner, the better!

Japan, Kawaguchiko: 22 Nov 2008, looking south to the north façade of Kawaguchiko Station (on the Fujikyu Kawaguchiko Line, terminal station, moving only to the left (southeast)), and the northern side of Mount Fuji (3,776 m, 1707 last eruption).

Bibliography

"The Histories" by Polybius
"Discours de la Méthode" by René Descartes
"Meditationes de prima philosophia" by René Descartes
"Philosophiae Naturalis Principia Mathematica" by Isaac Newton
Chinese encyclopedia Gujin Tushu Jicheng (Imperial
Enciclopaedia)
"Encyclopédie" by Jean-Baptiste le Rond d'Alembert and Denis
Diderot
"Encyclopaedia Britannica" by over 4,400 contributors
"Encyclopedia Americana" by Francis Lieber
"Grand Larousse encyclopédique en 24 volumes" by Albert
Ducrocq
Nobel Prize Organization
"The Cambridge History of Medicine", edited by Roy Porter
"Great Russian Encyclopedia" by Yury Osipov
"Encyclopedia of China"
"Enciclopedia Italiana di Scienze, Lettere ed Arti" (35 volume), by
Giovanni Treccani
Concise Oxford Dictionary of Opera
"Allgemeine Encyclopädie der Wissenschaften und Künste" by
Johann Samuel Ersch und Johann Gottfried Gruber
Grove Dictionary of Music and Musicians
"Gran Enciclopedia de España"
Other sources include: UPI, CNBC, AP, Nasdaq, Reuters, EDGAR,
AFP, Recode, Europa Press, Bloomberg News, Fox News, USA,
Deutsche Presse-Agentur, MSNBC, BBC, Australian Associated
Press, Agência Brasil, The Canadian Press (La Presse Canadienne),
Middle East News Agency, Baltic News Service, Suomen
Tietotoimisto, Athens-Macedonian News Agency, Asian News
International, Inter Press Service, Kyodo News, Notimex,
Algemeen Nederlands Persbureau, AGERPRES, Newsis,
Tidningarnas Telegrambyrå, Swiss Telegraphic Agency, Central
News Agency, ANKA news agency, Agenzia Fides

Michael M. Dediu is also the author of these books (which can be found on Amazon.com):

1. Aphorisms and quotations – with examples and explanations
2. Axioms, aphorisms and quotations – with examples and explanations
3. 100 Great Personalities and their Quotations
4. Professor Petre P. Teodorescu – A Great Mathematician and Engineer
5. Professor Ioan Goia – A Dedicated Engineering Professor
6. Venice (Venezia) – a new perspective. A short presentation with photographs
7. La Serenissima (Venice) - a new photographic perspective. A short presentation with many photos
8. Grand Canal – Venice. A new photographic viewpoint. A short presentation with many photos
9. Piazza San Marco – Venice. A different photographic view. A short presentation with many photos
10. Roma (Rome) - La Città Eterna. A new photographic view. A short presentation with many photos
11. Why is Rome so Fascinating? A short presentation with many photos
12. Rome, Boston and Helsinki. A short photographic presentation
13. Rome and Tokyo – two captivating cities. A short photographic presentation
14. Beautiful Places on Earth – A new photographic presentation
15. From Niagara Falls to Mount Fuji via Rome - A novel photographic presentation
16. From the USA and Canada to Italy and Japan - A fresh photographic presentation
17. Paris – Why So Many Call This City Mon Amour - A lovely photographic presentation
18. The City of Light – Paris (La Ville-Lumière) - A kaleidoscopic photographic presentation
19. Paris (Lutetia Parisiorum) – the romance capital of the world - A kaleidoscopic photographic view
20. Paris and Tokyo – a joyful photographic presentation. With a preamble about the Universe

21. From USA to Japan via Canada – A cheerful photographic documentary

22. 200 Wonderful Places, In The Last 50 Years – A personal photographic documentary

23. Must see places in USA and Japan - A kaleidoscopic photographic documentary

24. Grandeurs of the World - A kaleidoscopic photographic documentary

25. Corneliu Leu – writer on the same wavelength as Mark Twain. An American viewpoint

26. From Berkeley to Pompeii via Rome – A kaleidoscopic photographic documentary

27. From America to Europe via Japan - A kaleidoscopic photographic documentary

28. Discover America and Japan - A photographic documentary

29. J. R. Lucas – philosopher on a creative parallel with Plato, An American viewpoint

30. From America to Switzerland via France - A photographic documentary

31. From Bretton Woods to New York via Cape Cod - A photographic documentary

32. Splendid Places on the Atlantic Coast of the U. S. A. - A photographic documentary

33. Fourteen nice Cities on three Continents - A photographic documentary

34. 17 Picturesque Cities on the World Map - A photographic documentary

35. Unforgettable Places from Four Continents including Trump buildings - A photographic documentary

36. Dediu Newsletter, Volume 1, Number 1, 6 December 2016 – Monthly news, review, comments and suggestions for a better and wiser world

37. Dediu Newsletter, Volume 1, Number 2, 6 January 2017 (available at www.derc.com).

38. Dediu Newsletter, Volume 1, Number 3, 6 February 2017 (available at www.derc.com).

39. London and Greenwich, A photographic documentary

40. Dediu Newsletter, Volume 1, Number 4, 6 March 2017 (available also at www.derc.com).

41. Dediu Newsletter, Volume 1, Number 5, 6 April 2017 (available also at www.derc.com).

42. Dediu Newsletter, Volume 1, Number 6, 6 May 2017 (available also at www.derc.com).

43. Dediu Newsletter, Volume 1, Number 7, 6 June 2017 (available also at www.derc.com).

44. London, Oxford and Cambridge, A photographic documentary

45. Dediu Newsletter, Volume 1, Number 8, 6 July 2017 (available also at www.derc.com).

46. Dediu Newsletter, Volume 1, Number 9, 6 August 2017 (available also at www.derc.com).

47. Dediu Newsletter, Volume 1, Number 10, 6 September 2017 (available also at www.derc.com).

48. Three Great Professors: President Woodrow Wilson, Historian Germán Arciniegas, Mathematician Gheorghe Vrănceanu, A chronological and photographic documentary

49. Dediu Newsletter, Volume 1, Number 11, 6 October 2017 (available also at www.derc.com).

50 Dediu Newsletter, Volume 1, Number 12, 6 November 2017 (available also at www.derc.com).

51 Dediu Newsletter, Volume 2, Number 1 (13), 6 December 2017 (available also at www.derc.com).

52 Two Great Leaders: Augustus and George Washington, A chronological and photographic documentary

53. Dediu Newsletter, Volume 2, Number 2 (14), 6 January 2018 (available also at www.derc.com).

54. Newton, Benjamin Franklin, and Gauss, A chronological and photographic documentary

55. Dediu Newsletter, Volume 2, Number 3 (15), 6 February 2018 (available also at www.derc.com).

56. 2017: World Top Events, But Many Little Known, A chronological and photographic documentary

57. Dediu Newsletter, Volume 2, Number 4 (16), 6 March 2018 (available also at www.derc.com).

58. Vergilius, Horatius, Ovidius, and Shakespeare, A chronological and photographic documentary.

59. Dediu Newsletter, Volume 2, Number 5 (17), 6 April 2018 (available also at www.derc.com).

60. Dediu Newsletter, Volume 2, Number 6 (18), 6 May 2018 (available also at www.derc.com).
61. Vivaldi, Bach, Mozart, and Verdi, A chronological and photographic documentary
62. Dediu Newsletter, Volume 2, Number 7 (19), 6 June 2018 (available also at www.derc.com).
63. Dediu Newsletter, Volume 2, Number 8 (20), 6 July 2018 (available also at www.derc.com).
64. Dediu Newsletter, Volume 2, Number 9 (21), 6 August 2018 (available also at www.derc.com).
65. World History, a new perspective - A chronological and photographic documentary.
66. World Humor History with over 100 Jokes, a new perspective - A chronological and photographic documentary
67. Dediu Newsletter, Vol 2, N 10 (22), 6 September 2018
68. Dediu Newsletter, Vol 2, N 11 (23), 6 October 2018
69. Da Vinci, Michelangelo, Rembrandt, Rodin - A chronological and photographic documentary
70. Dediu Newsletter, Vol 2, N 12 (24), 6 November 2018
71. Dediu Newsletter, Vol 3, N 1 (25), 6 December 2018
72. From Euclid to Edison - revelries in the last 75 years - A chronological and photographic documentary
73. Dediu Newsletter, Vol 3, N 2 (26), 6 January 2019
74. Socrates to Churchill - Aphorisms celebrated after 1960 - A chronological and photographic documentary
75. Dediu Newsletter Vol 3, Number 3 (27), 6 February 2019
76. Hippocrates to Fleming: Medicine History celebrated after 1943 - A chronological and photographic documentary
77. Dediu Newsletter, Volume 3, Number 4 (28), 6 March 2019
78. Dediu Newsletter, Volume 3, Number 5 (29), 6 April 2019
79. Archimedes to Ford: Invention History celebrated after 1943 - A chronological and photographic documentary
80. Dediu Newsletter, Volume 3, Number 6 (30), 6 May 2019
81. Sutherland to Pavarotti: Great Singers History - A chronological and photographic documentary
82. Dediu Newsletter, Volume 3, Number 7 (31), 6 June 2019
83. Dediu Newsletter, Volume 3, Number 8 (32), 6 July 2019
84. Augustus to Rockefeller: History of the Wealthiest People - A chronological and photographic documentary

85. Dediu Newsletter, Volume 3, Number 9 (33), 6 August 2019
86 – Pythagoras to Fermi: History of Science - A chronological and photographic documentary
87. Dediu Newsletter, Volume 3, Number 10 (34), 6 September 2019

Italy, Cividale del Friuli: 3 Nov 2009, on Corso Paolino d'Aquileia, on the bridge of Iacopo da Bissone (1442, 50 m by 3.6 m, height 22.5 m, rock) over Natisone River (flowing to the back), 150 m southeast of Palazzo Comunale, looking west to il Campanile (up right) of Chiesa di San Francesco.

Michael M. Dediu is the editor of these books (also on Amazon.com):

1. Sophia Dediu: The life and its torrents – Ana. In Europe around 1920
2. Proceedings of the 4th International Conference "Advanced Composite Materials Engineering" COMAT 2012
3. Adolf Shvedchikov: I am an eternal child of spring – poems in English, Italian, French, German, Spanish and Russian
4. Adolf Shvedchikov: Life's Enigma – poems in English, Italian and Russian
5. Adolf Shvedchikov: Everyone wants to be HAPPY – poems in English, Spanish and Russian
6. Adolf Shvedchikov: My Life, My Love – poems in English, Italian and Russian
7. Adolf Shvedchikov: I am the gardener of love – poems in English and Russian
8. Adolf Shvedchikov: Amaretta di Saronno – poems in English and Russian
9. Adolf Shvedchikov: A Russian Rediscovers America
10. Adolf Shvedchikov: Parade of Life - poems in English and Russian
11. Adolf Shvedchikov: Overcoming Sorrow - poems in English and Russian
12. Sophia Dediu: Sophia meets Japan
13. Corneliu Leu: Roosevelt, Churchill, Stalin and Hitler: Their surprising role in Eastern Europe in 1944
14. Proceedings of the 5th International Conference "Computational Mechanics and Virtual Engineering" COMEC 2013
15. Georgeta Simion – Potanga: Beyond Imagination: A Thought-provoking novel inspired from mid-20th century events
16. Ana Dediu: The poetry of my life in Europe and The USA
17. Ana Dediu: The Four Graces
18. Proceedings of the 5th International Conference "Advanced Composite Materials Engineering" COMAT 2014
19. Sophia Dediu: Chocolate Cook Book: Is there such a thing as too much chocolate?

20. Sorin Vlase: Mechanical Identifiability in Automotive Engineering

21. Gabriel Dima: The Evolution of the Aerostructures – Concept and Technologies

22. Proceedings of the 6th International Conference "Computational Mechanics and Virtual Engineering" COMEC 2015

23. Sophia Dediu: Cook Book 1 A-B-C Common sense cooking

24. Sophia Dediu: Dim Sum Spring Festival

25. Ana Dediu and Sophia Dediu: Europe in 1985: A chronological and photographic documentary

26 Stefan Staretu: Europe: Serbian Despotate of Srem and the Romanian area. Between the 14th and the 16th Centuries

USA, Cambridge: 26 Sep 2010, Dante Alighieri (1265-1321, poet, statesman, language theorist) Society of Massachusetts, Italian Cultural Center, on Hampshire Street at Cardinal Medeiros Ave., 800 m north of MIT.

Venere (Venus) Italica, 1810, by Antonio Canova, 53, (1757 – 1822, aged 65, sculptor from Venezia), a carved Carrara marble sculpture, 1.75 m, commissioned by Napoleon Bonaparte, 41, (1769 – 1821, aged 52).

www.ingramcontent.com/pod-product-compliance
Lightning Source LLC
Chambersburg PA
CBHW041309210326
41599CB00003B/37